Production planning and control

Production planning and control

Production planning and control

W. Bolton

Longman
Scientific &
Technical

Longman Scientific & Technical
Longman Group UK Limited
Longman House, Burnt Mill, Harlow
Essex CM20 2JE, England
and Associated Companies throughout the world

First published 1994

British Library Cataloguing in Publication Data
A catalogue entry for this title is available from the British Library.

ISBN 0–582–22820–4

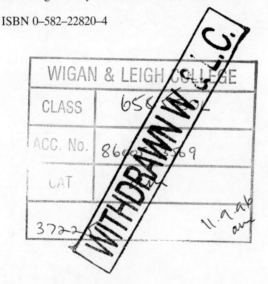
Set by 8 in 10/11 pt Times
Printed in Malaysia by TCP

Contents

Preface

This book aims to give the reader an appreciation and understanding of

1   the ways in which manufacturing companies are organised,
2   the nature and diversity of engineering products,
3   the organisation of production,
4   the planning and control of production.

The book more than covers the BTEC units Control of manufacture U83/188 and Production planning and control U83/189 and has been written primarily for use in BTEC Higher National Certificate and Higher National Diploma programmes in Mechanical and Production Engineering.

While it is recognised that computer programs can be used for many of the topics considered in the book, it was felt that the emphasis in the book should be on the establishment of the basic principles by working things out 'by hand'. This was felt to be more appropriate in a text concerned with the introduction of basic principles and would then enable the reader to use computer programs intelligently and be more able to interpret the results with understanding.

Each chapter includes revision questions and case problems. Outlines of answers to all revision questions are given. References are included throughout the text, and in a further reading section, to texts and standards which can be used to extend the coverage provided by the text. It is recognised that the entire subject could be taught through assignments based on a real company or a 'paper' company and this issue is addressed in the appendix to the book.

W. Bolton

1 The manufacturing organisation

1.1 The manufacturing organisation

Production can be defined as the act of providing something which somebody wants. This might be a material item or a service. Thus an organisation making cars or a bank providing financial services can both be thought of as being involved in production. For this book, production is restricted to the production of material products. The term *manufacturing* is often used for such forms of production.

A production organisation which has a material output can be considered to be a system where the inputs and outputs may take one or more of the following forms:

1 Raw materials being converted from their initially discovered state into a material which can be used to produce some item, e.g. an organisation turning iron ore into sheet steel.
2 Materials being converted into components or parts, e.g. an organisation converting steel into car engine piston rods.
3 Parts and components being converted into assembled goods, e.g. cars being assembled.

A car manufacturer might buy in some made components, make some of its own from bought-in materials, and assemble cars using these components. Such an organisation is thus of form 3 with some aspects of 2.

1.1.1 Objectives of a manufacturing organisation

The objectives of an organisation are the purposes for which it is in existence. The prime objective of an organisation in the private sector can generally be considered to be the *maximisation of profit*. An important distinction needs to be made between maximisation of profit and minimisation of cost, as one does not necessarily imply the other. Cheap, shoddy, articles may be a consequence of cost minimisation and may not result in the maximisation of profit that could occur with higher cost but better quality goods.

The private sector is that part of the economic system which is independent of government control, organisations in the public sector being generally concerned with the prime objective of the maxmisation of national welfare.

Maximising profit for a manufacturing organisation can mean, in its simplest context, getting orders and executing them to the satisfaction of the customers. This requires products to be in demand and be competitive in price, quality and delivery. Without this the organisation will not survive. To achieve such objectives, production has to be efficiently organised.

The policies of an organisation are the means by which its objectives are to be achieved. The objectives and the policies form a plan for the organisation. Thus, in simple terms, a production department might, as part of the organisation plan, have to plan to produce x units per week initially, increasing to y by the end of the year, using the existing number of workers with new plant for one of the operations being introduced during the year and the existing workforce being trained accordingly.

1.2 Structure of manufacturing organisations

With the exception of very small manufacturing organisations there will be invariably some division of labour among the employees. This means that some employees will specialise in one aspect of the work of the organisation while others specialise in other aspects. The result of such a division of labour is a need for an organisational structure through which decisions are made, instructions transmitted and communication occurs. This generally involves a subdivision of the personnel into different departments, each department having a specific function or group of related functions. There are a number of ways in which an organisation can be subdivided.

1 *By business function* The employees are grouped according to the business function they are involved with, e.g. all those concerned with production being in the production department, those concerned with marketing in the marketing department.
2 *By product* All the employees concerned with the same product are grouped together, e.g. the car division and the lorry division.

3 *By process*   The employees are grouped so that the departments each provide a particular type of process, e.g. a printing department, a foundry department.

4 *By customer*   The employees are grouped according to the particular territory in which the customers are located, e.g. the south of England, or by the type of customer, e.g. governments, wholesalers.

5 *By geography*   The organisation may need to provide services in a number of different regions and thus have departments in the regions.

Organisations often have more than one form of departmentalisation. Probably the most common form, however, is by business function with all those engaged in the same business function being grouped together. The major departments in such a manufacturing organisation tend to be production, design and development, finance, marketing and personnel.

1 *Production department*   This has the responsibility for all the activities associated with the receipt of raw materials/bought-in products and their conversion into the end-products for sale.

2 *Design and development department*   This involves the research, development and design of new products and modifications to existing products.

3 *Finance department*   This department has the responsibility for running the financial affairs of the organisation. This involves maintaining accounts, costing services and products, and preparing financial forecasts.

4 *Marketing department*   This has the responsibility for all the activities associated with selling the organisation's products. This involves market research, demand forecasting, promoting products by advertising, selecting distributive outlets, etc.

5 *Personnel department*   This department has the responsibility for labour recruitment and selection, training, industrial relations, working conditions, safety and health, welfare, etc.

The work of any one department is often interrelated with that of other departments. Thus, for the production department:

1 The interaction with the design and development department might be in regard to the supply of the design of new products or modifications for existing products, manufacturing standards and quality, equipment design.

2 The interaction with the finance department is likely to be in regard to production budgets, equipment replacement decisions, costing of products.

3 The marketing department might supply demand forecasts, production schedules to satisfy delivery dates, and plan production capacity.

4 The personnel department will have an involvement with labour recruitment, training, safety and health.

1.2.1 Organisation chart

The *organisation chart* shows the *lines of authority* within an organisation. *Authority* is the right to make decisions, give orders and direct the work of others. Figure 1.1 shows a form of organisation chart that might be adopted for a medium-size organisation where the employees have been grouped according to their functions, e.g. there is a production department in which all the production workers are grouped, a design and development department in which all the workers involved in design and development are grouped. In essence, the organisation chart shows by its lines a hierarchy headed by the chief executive and extending down through the various levels of managers and supervisors to the manual and clerical workers. A small organisation is likely to have fewer layers of management than a large one.

A person is said to have *line authority* if he, or she, appears within the line of authority in the organisation chart. However, in addition to the line relationships, there are numerous other relationships involving the co-ordination of activities across line boundaries.

An important point is the distinction between *authority* and *responsibility*. A manager might delegate some authority to a subordinate so that he, or she, can make some decisions, give orders and direct the work of others. The subordinate has thus some degree of authority but is accountable to the manager for the performance of the assigned tasks. The ultimate responsibility, however, still lies with the manager. Authority can be delegated but responsibility cannot.

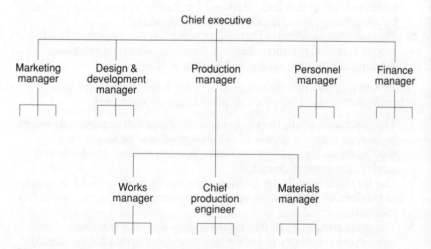

Figure 1.1 The basic form of an organisation chart

Thus, with the organisation chart shown in Figure 1.1, the chief executive can delegate authority down the chart but the overall responsibility for the organisation still lies with the chief executive.

1.2.2 Matrix structure

Figure 1.1 is just one form of structure that can be adopted by an organisation. The organisation of a company in functional lines can present communication problems if the lines are long or if a particular project needs co-operation between employees in a number of lines. Where a company is engaged on a number of separate projects, a *matrix management structure* might be used. With this form of structure a group of project departments is superimposed over the functional line structure. A manager is put in charge of each project and is given the authority and responsibility for completing the project. He, or she, is assigned workers from a number of functional departments for the duration of the project. On completion of the project the workers return to their functional departments. This form of structure enables a self-contained department to draw on a range of skills and give its continuous and undivided attention to a project. The advent of each new project can result in a different grouping of workers and so the matrix form provides a flexible structure which adjusts to the demands put on it.

The matrix form of structure enables what is termed *simultaneous engineering* or *concurrent engineering*. The traditional process for the introduction of, say, a new product is likely to involve a number of functional departments: for example, the marketing department might find out what functions are required of the new product, the design department might then produce a design, and the production department might develop the production methods. There is what might be termed a serial development of the project, with each aspect being completed and passed from one department to another for successive stages in the development. The matrix form of structure does, however, allow all the workers, whatever their functional departments, to be grouped under one head for the duration of the project of the product development. A multi-disciplinary team is then involved, rather than each discipline working independently of the other. There is concurrent development of all the aspects of the product development rather than the serial approach which is typical of the functional department form of structure. Concurrent engineering has the potential to reduce the time taken to develop a product and increase the quality.

1.2.3 Span of authority

The term *span of authority* is used for the number or persons directly reporting to an individual. The determining factor is the demands on the manager's time. The more routine the tasks of the subordinates, the more people that can be managed. A figure often quoted for the typical span is 7; however, it does need to be realised that the optimum number will depend on many factors, e.g. similarity and complexity of the functions supervised, geographic closeness of the subordinates, degree of control required. A small span makes for more efficient communication and control between manager and subordinates, but is expensive. Larger spans of control save money but may make it impossible for a manager to exercise effective control.

The fact that there is a limit to the number of people who can report directly to any one individual is one reason why a large organisation requires more layers of management than a small organisation. If an organisation had, say, 4000 employees, and if the span of authority was 4 at each level, then the numbers at each descending level would be

1, 4, 16, 64, 256, 1024, 4096

– a total of 7 levels. If, however, the span of authority was 8 at each level, the numbers would be

1, 8, 64, 512, 4096

– a total of 5 levels. There is thus a direct relationship between the span of control and the number of levels within the organisation hierarchy.

1.3 The functions of managers

In general, managers tend to carry out certain basic functions within an organisation.

1 *Planning*   This is the setting of objectives and targets, making predictions and planning for future demands.
2 *Organising*   The manager has to organise his, or her, subordinates. This requires determining, within the overall plan of the organisation, the activities that should be undertaken and how these should be carried out. It also involves delegating authority and establishing channels of communication.
3 *Co-ordinating*   This is the directing of the efforts of subordinates so that their efforts all tend towards the same end, namely the achievement of the laid down plan.
4 *Controlling*   This is the checking of how the actual performance of subordinates compares with that planned and making adjustments with the aim of changing performance so that the plan is achieved.
5 *Leading*   The manager has to provide the necessary leadership for the subordinates.
6 *Staffing*   The manager has to determine the staffing policy for those subordinate to him or her. This involves a consideration of not only numbers of staff but their skill requirements.

1.3.1   Co-ordination

Co-ordination is the process of gathering together the efforts of individuals and groups engaged in a number of interdependent activities to ensure that all their efforts are aimed in the same direction and there is a smooth operation. For example, in the making of some product all the materials must have been ordered in time to be in stock when they are required, the workforce must work at the appropriate rate to ensure that the parts each makes are ready when required by others, etc.

The following are some of the methods that can be used to achieve co-ordination:

1 *Targets*   Targets are set for each department/section/employee and if these are all achieved then the overall plan is attained and hence co-ordination has occurred.
2 *Rules or procedures*   Each employee is expected to carry out tasks in a prescribed way and rate. Effectively there are sets of standards which have to be met.
3 *Supervision*   Supervision of the activities might be undertaken by some interdepartmental committee, or special liaison people or team.
4 *Grouping*   The co-ordination of all the activities associated with a particular product can be enhanced if departments are structured, at this level, by product rather than by business function. All the individuals working on the product are in one group rather than spread across a number of departments.

1.3.2 Controlling

Controlling is the checking of how the actual performance of subordinates compares with that planned, and making adjustments with the aim of changing performance so that the plan is achieved. This can be illustrated by considering the problem of maintaining the temperature in a centrally heated room by means of a thermostat. The *objective* in this instance can be considered to be the obtaining of the required temperature, with the *policy* being to do this by switching a heater on or off. The objective and the policy constitute the plan. The thermostat is the controller. The temperature is sensed/measured using an appropriate transducer and communicated to the thermostat where it is compared with that planned. If the temperature falls below that planned, the thermostat switches the heater on; if it rises above, it switches the heater off. The vital elements in the temperature control system are the plan, measurement, comparison of the actual temperature with that planned, and then corrective action.

In an organisation, controlling can be considered to have the following elements:

1 *Planning*   The required performance is determined.
2 *Communicating*   The plan is communicated to those concerned.
3 *Measurement*   The actual performance is measured, e.g. by completed products, time sheets, material requisitions.

4 *Comparison* The performance is compared with the plan.
5 *Reporting* Deviations from the plan are reported to a supervisor/ manager.
6 *Corrective action* When performance is not in accord with the plan then corrective action has to be initiated. This will require a clear identification of the problem and the real reasons for its occurrence. Is it a one-off occurrence or a trend in performance? It might be that the plan itself is in need of revision or perhaps training and development are called for, or the problem may be poor staffing.

To illustrate the control activity, consider a production plan where 1000 components have to be produced per day with no more than 10 rejects. If measurement of the output each day indicates that, say, 1000 components are being produced but there are 20 rejects, then corrective action is required. The corrective action might be the adjustment of a machine or special training for an operator. If, however, the high number of rejects persists then there might be a need to reconsider the plan.

Examples of general areas of control are budgetary control and production control. Budgetary control is probably the most significant means of exercising control. A financial budget, prepared on the basis of forecasts of intended activity, constitutes the plan against which income and expenditure are compared. Such control can be exercised at the overall organisation level, at departmental level and at subdepartment levels. The object of budgetary control is to keep control of the organisation finances. Production control might have the objectives of ensuring that competitive delivery dates are offered for products, customers' orders are delivered on time, effective use is made of all the plant and manpower, there is not too high a build-up of stocks or too much work in progress. Areas of administration within this might include quality control, manufacturing cost control, stock control and maintenance control.

1.4 Communication

Communication is the means by which every individual in an organisation is linked and can be both formal and informal. It is the means by which all instructions, information, opinions and attitudes are transmitted between individuals, whether it be from the chief executive to a manager, a manager to another manager, a supervisor to a worker, one supervisor to another, or worker to worker. Thus in terms of the organisation chart, there needs to be both vertical and horizontal communication.

It is necessary to recognise that communication is not just about transmitting information; effective communication does not occur

unless the recipient of the communication understands its meaning.
The stages of communication can be considered to be:

1 conceiving the message that is to be communicated
2 encoding the message into a suitable form for transmission, e.g. the
   written word, drawing
3 selecting the communication channel, e.g. writing, speaking
4 receiving and decoding the message
5 interpreting the message
6 using some feedback mechanism to indicate that the message has
   been received, decoded and interpreted.

Good communication is vital for efficient running of an organisation.
How often in an organisation are the comments heard: 'Nobody told
me that . . .' or 'I did not realise that we were expected to do that'?
Barriers to effective communication can occur, for example, as a result
of: imprecise language being used; specialists using terms which are
not understood by the recipient; the number of people through which a
message has to be passed before it reaches the one who has to act on
the message; status differences between people which result, for
example, in a manager not realising that a subordinate has not
understood the communication.

Poor communication can lead to problems. For instance,
misunderstandings can lead to mistakes, wastage, accidents, confusion,
etc. Poor communication from management can lead to employees
becoming frustrated, with a drop in morale, with consequent drops in
productivity and even unrest and strikes. Poor communication up the
line can mean that managers are not aware of problems and
grievances, with a possible consequence of worker dissatisfaction and
poor co-operation.

Formal communications are those that can be considered to be
official by the organisation. They include the orders down the line of
command, committees, liaison groups, written communications, and
company publications. Informal communications are not usually
officially sanctioned but many of them are necessary for the effective
running of the organisation. They include the 'grape vine' and informal
discussions between employees in different departments or within
departments.

The longer the line along which information is to be passed, the
longer the time factor and the greater the chance of misunderstandings
occurring. Thus a company making a diversity of products will often
seek to reduce the length of its communications lines by decentralising
the manufacture of products, though retaining overall financial control.
The layout of manufacturing facilities can also be used to reduce
communication lines. This is particularly evident with group layout
(see Chapter 3 for further details) where machines are grouped to
enable the workers operating them to deal with all the processes
involved in manufacturing some item or items that have similar

operating sequences. Most of the communication thus occurs within the group.

Problems

Revision questions

1 What is the purpose of an organisation chart and what factors determine its form?
2 Distinguish between the terms authority and responsibility.
3 Explain the need for good communication in an organisation and ways that might be used to achieve this.
4 Outline the main functions of managers.
5 Explain the need for, and methods of obtaining, co-ordination in an organisation.
6 Explain the basic elements inherent in organisation control systems.

Case problems

7 John had been working as a supervisor in a machine shop in a large company when it closed and he was made redundant. With his redundancy money and a loan from the bank, he set up a small company with a few workers to make machine parts, thereby filling a gap in the market left when the large organisation closed.
   (a) What would be the likely organisation chart for the company at this stage?
   (b) The company did well and expanded, taking on more workers. John found that he had to spend more and more time supervising and was not able to also chase orders, keep the accounts and order materials. What would be the likely organisation chart to which the company could now evolve? What type of problems might John have faced if the organisation did not change?
   (c) The company did well enough to be able to take over some small companies. These were located in other towns. What now might be a likely organisation chart?
   (d) As the company evolves, what control mechanisms might John have to put in place?
   (e) As the company evolves, what communication problems might be experienced?
8 The college feels that there could be benefits in setting up a college-company involving the full-time students from a number of courses and departments so that they could gain some realistic experience of what it would be like to operate in a company environment. The proposed product is a car tool set (you might like to consider this question in relation to other products). Produce a plan for the organisation of the company, paying particular attention to the functions required, and how effective communication and control can be exercised.

2 Controlling

2.1 The control process

Controlling is the checking of how actual performance compares with that planned and making adjustments with the aim of ensuring that the plan is achieved (see section 1.3.2 for a preliminary discussion). The control process can be considered to involve planning and communicating the required standards/targets, measuring performance against these standards/targets, identifying deviations and taking corrective action.

A technique that is increasingly adopted to set the standards/targets is management by objectives.

2.1.1 Management by objectives

The term *management by objectives* is a technique by which superiors and subordinates jointly set the targets for the subordinates and periodically assess progress towards these targets. Management by objectives involves subordinates participating in setting objectives. This technique may be used at a high level in an organisation to determine overall objectives and at a lower level between, say, a production manager and a subordinate or subordinates to determine production targets. The technique may be used as an organisation-wide policy or perhaps from just some aspects.

Management by objectives when adopted as an organisation-wide policy is likely to take the following form.

1 Organisation objectives are set.
2 Departmental objectives are set by discussions between department heads and their superiors.
3 Departmental heads then discuss departmental objectives with their supervisor subordinates so that they develop their own objectives.
4 Individual objectives are then discussed between individuals and their supervisors.
5 There are periodic review meetings at each level to monitor and analyse progress towards the objectives. This then results in feedback up the chain, with possible modification of the organisation objectives.

One of the main advantages of this technique is that those concerned know what their jobs are, what standards of achievement are required, and how they are getting on. Participation in the decision making means less conflict and mistrust and a greater feeling of being part of an organisation. Adopted across the organisation it forces on management a continuous examination of what it is doing and the way it is doing it. A problem with this approach is that common agreement may lead to targets that are too low, since those concerned know that they can achieve those targets and so appear to be successful. It can also be very time consuming, at the expense of productive work. It can also lead to a dilution of managerial input through the opinions of those unskilled in decision making and without the necessary perspective.

2.2 Fitting controls to the task

Control systems can take the form of quality control charts, inventory control charts, monthly sales figures, budget reports, etc. But whatever the form the problem that has to be faced is how much control should be exercised? Where the employees have very routine, predictable tasks the control is generally fairly tight with little self-control being expected. Control is then often through imposed rules and procedures. Where the employees have very unpredictable tasks the control is generally found to be fairly loose with managers depending a great deal on self-control. The focus is then on the outcome, rather than on how it is achieved.

2.2.1 Management by exception

Management by exception involves only significant deviations from standards/targets being brought to a manager's attention. The aim of this is to conserve the manager's time by ensuring that he or she is only involved in important matters, and is not troubled with control reports when the performance is in line with the planned standards/targets. At lower levels of management, this approach is often used for routine day-to-day control.

2.3 Management information systems

Management information systems are designed to provide rapidly the information management needs for control and effective decision making. Information may be gathered through a range of information systems, e.g. quality control reports, monthly sales figures, budget reports, inventory control reports, etc. With a manual information system the data, on sheets of paper, is gathered in and processed by clerks extracting the information from it and putting it into the form required by management.

A manual information system might involve, for the production department, such documents as:

1. a budget for the production department and associated control documents enabling actual performance to be compared with budgeted performance
2. a works order, which passes information from the sales department to the production department about orders received
3. an operation sheet, which is a statement of the production processes, equipment, materials, production aids, times allocated, etc.
4. a job schedule, which is a plan of the production process and how it is to be broken down into its constituent tasks
5. a loading schedule, which outlines the tasks to be undertaken by a specific operator or machine
6. an operator's work sheet, which gives the record of the work completed by an operator
7. material requisitions to the materials store
8. quality control charts, which give the results of product inspection.

The term *management information system*, however, is generally used to mean a computer-based system which integrates all or most of the organisation's information systems and monitors activities throughout the organisation. Data can then, for example, be reported direct from the production process by means of transducers connected on-line to key production equipment and by means of data being keyed in manually at terminals located at the information source. The advantages of a computer-based system over a manual system is that the processing time before data is available to management is reduced, and also the volume of information that can be handled is increased.

A simple illustration of the differences between a manual- and computer-operated information system can be gained by considering a simple situation of a supermarket. When a computerised information system is in use, the sales assistant scans the bar code of an item when it is sold. This automatically identifies the item and its price. For each item the customer is purchasing, such entries are made on a computer file. At the end, the computer determines the total cost and produces a printed receipt for the customer. However, the computer is also logging the information against each of the items so that the shop manager can have a printed report of sales of each item, which can also trigger off orders for stock replacement. In addition, it can send information to the headquarters of the store group to enable overall management decisions to be made. Now consider what the situation would be in the absence of the computer. The sales assistant might have to add up the cost of each item so that the customer can be told the price. The shop manager can only know what has been sold and in what quantities by assigning staff to count stock and keep records of stock movement. Orders then have to be made when this information is analysed by someone. The store manager has to compile all reports to headquarters. The main difference between the computerised and manual forms of operation are, in this case, the speed with which information is available and the quantity of information that is readily available.

In designing a management information system the following factors have to be considered.

1   What are the information needs of the organisation? Thus, the production manager might need to know what jobs are being handled in the production department and what their state of completion is, what jobs are due to arrive and when, what the stocks of materials are, etc. The information needs in an organisation will differ from level to level. Senior management is likely to want information relevant to policy making and strategic planning; middle management, information relevant to control; lower management, information relevant to the maintenance and implementation of daily activities, such as production scheduling.

2   What are the channels of information flow? There will be need for information flow down the management levels, up the levels and horizontally between sections and departments. Figure 2.1 shows some of the main paths of information flow that are likely to occur in a manufacturing organisation.

3   In what form is the information required? In order to discern trends, a manager might, for instance, want information presented in the form of a graph. The extent to which summaries are required is likely to increase the more senior the management.

4   How is the information to be presented? Does it need, for instance, to be in the form of a printout or on a visual display unit (VDU)?

The information fed into the system may be processed on-line or as a batch. An on-line system means that the data is processed continuously with the minimum of delay. Batch processing means that the data is accumulated over a period, e.g. a day, and then processed. Errors can occur in data input. Such errors can be minimised if data is collected in as simple a form as possible, there is the minimum delay possible in reporting data, and the person responsible for the activity generating

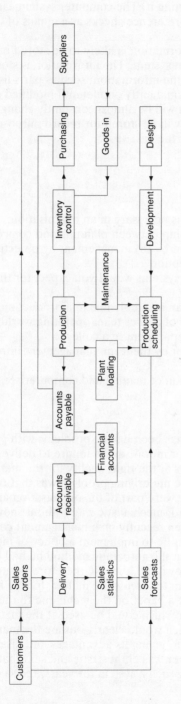

Figure 2.1 Information flow

the data is the one reporting it. The computer system can institute format, range and cross-reference checks as a means of detecting errors.

A large amount of information is likely to be stored in a management information system. The information is stored as coded data elements. Some of the information, such as parts listing of a product, will be kept permanently on file until modified or discarded. Some of the information will be almost constantly changing, e.g. work-in-progress, while some will be stored for record purposes, e.g. monthly sales figures for the past year.

Problems

Revision questions

1 Explain why control is necessary in an organisation.
2 Explain the relationship between planning and control.
3 Explain what is meant by (a) management by objectives and (b) management by exception.
4 What sort of control systems would you expect for the following situations?
   (a) A supervisor of an assembly line in a production plant.
   (b) A sales manager of a sales team operating worldwide.
   (c) The head of a department in a college.
5 Explain what is meant by the term 'management information systems'.
6 Compare the operation of manual and computerised processing of information.

Case problems

7 The ABC company has been having problems with poor communications, poor morale and a failure to deliver the right quantities of products at the right quality for the market. The chief executive felt that the underlying problem was that the employees did not feel that they were part of the organisation and did their jobs in a non-involved, mechanistic way without showing any initiative. Having been recently on a management course he felt that the answer might be to implement a policy of management by objectives rather than the autocratic method he had been using of directing decisions down the line. He therefore brought together the management team to discuss the matter, having arranged for a consultant to present a paper on the technique to them.
   (a) Develop a paper which could be used at the management team meeting and which would clearly outline the management by objectives system, giving its advantages and disadvantages.
   (b) The sales manager was enthusiastic and said that he had been virtually running such a system for years, the sales

representatives having been largely left to their own devices. Present the argument that the sales manager has not completely understood the technique.

(c) The production manager was not enthusiastic, feeling that such a scheme was completely inappropriate for the production line where he felt that it was necessary for him to lay down the standards required. It was, however, pointed out that the production line workers were currently on a go-slow because of misunderstandings concerning new techniques being introduced. Present the case for the production manager considering management by objectives.

8 A small manufacturing company is considering introducing a management information system.

(a) Acting as a consultant to the company, prepare a paper for presentation to their management team. The paper should outline the information that needs to be gathered before a system can be designed.

(b) The company makes goods to order, the goods being components designed, specified and required by a large company. What information paths are likely to occur between the customer and the company?

(c) The company has a finance department. What information paths are likely to occur between it, other sections within the company, and customers and suppliers?

9 The following is the situation in company DEF which makes products in batches for stock, orders from cutomers then being delivered from stock. Draw a diagram indicating the flow of information.

(a) Production control instructs the manufacturing section to make certain batches.

(b) The manufacturing section instructs stores that certain raw materials will be required.

(c) The stores section instructs the purchasing section to place orders to bring its stocks up to required levels.

(d) The purchasing section orders the materials from its list of approved suppliers, after checking delivery dates.

(e) The supplier sends the materials to the stores.

(f) Stores advise the accounts section that the materials have been received.

(g) The accounts section receives an invoice from the supplier.

(h) The accounts section pays the supplier.

(i) The stores section advises the manufacturing section that it has the materials in store.

(j) The manufacturing section draws the materials from the store.

(k) The manufacturing section produces the required batches and sends them to stores section.

(l) The manufacturing section advises production control that the batches have been completed.

(m) Production control advises the sales section that the products are now available for sale.

(n) The sales section receives orders from customers.

(o) The sales section advises despatch of the orders.

(p) Despatch obtains the products from store.

(q) Despatch sends the products to the customer.

(r) Despatch advises accounts that the products have been sent.

(s) Accounts bill the customer.

(t) The customer remits the money to accounts.

3 Production organisation

3.1 The production manager

The functions for which a production manager is responsible will depend on the nature of the products being manufactured. Typically they can be:

1 *Production planning and control*   This will involve planning, scheduling, loading, progressing and controlling. Scheduling is the working out of the routeing and timetabling of the various tasks associated with the production. Loading is the timetabling of the work for a single operator or machine. Progressing is the checking that all is proceeding to plan. Production control is concerned with ensuring that the production department meets its objectives.
2 *Production*   This involves the management of the production resources in order to ensure that production schedules are met and includes the manufacturing, assembly, materials stores and finished products store.
3 *Inspection*   This involves quality control, materials and components inward inspection and shop-floor inspection.
4 *Engineering*   This can include jig and tool design and the design tool room.
5 *Work study*   This involves method study and work measurement. Work study is a general term used to describe the systematic investigation of activities in order to improve the effectiveness of

the use of human and material resources. There are two main aspects of work study: method study, which involves finding the best way of doing a task; and work measurement, which is concerned with finding how long a task should take.

6 *Maintenance*   This will involve maintaining and replacing plant.

7 *Liaison*   There will need to be liaison with other departments, e.g. the sales department with regard to production schedules, the personnel department to ensure that suitable workers are hired and that appropriate training is given.

Figure 3.1 shows how a production department might be organised to enable the production manager to carry out the above functions. In some organisations the production manager might also be responsible for design and development. The larger the organisation the more subdivided the task will become to ensure an acceptable span of control for the manager/supervisor at each level.

3.2   Types of production

Production operations can be classified according to the degree of repetitiveness involved, with five basic types being identified.

1   Project
2   Jobbing
3   Batch
4   Flow
5   Process.

The *project* form is concerned with large-scale complex products and involves the allocation and co-ordination of large-scale inputs to achieve a unique product. For example, in a large civil engineering project to build a new factory, resources have to be allocated for the duration of the project.

Jobbing describes the situation where the whole of a product is considered as one operation and work is completed on each product before starting on the next. Such a form of production is concerned with making one, or a very small number, of unique items. This is likely to be in response to a customer's order and specification rather than production for stock. It could be, for example, a purpose-built piece of equipment for some plant. Jobbing requires tool adjustments and a production process specifically chosen to fit the unique requirements of the one-off product. It requires workers, plant and tools which are versatile since they may be called on to perform a variety of tasks. The amount of time spent on setting up and adjusting machines for a one-off product can be fairly extensive and, consequently, the cost per unit is usually high.

With the *batch* form of production, larger volumes of product are required than with jobbing. This is likely to be most economically

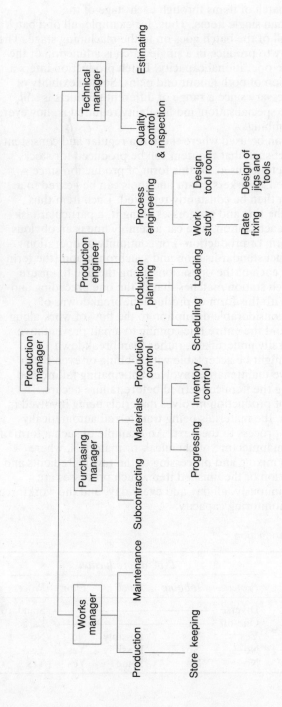

Figure 3.1 Organisation of a production department

tackled by taking a batch of items through each stage of the production, rather than single items. Thus, for example, all of a batch may be cast before all of the batch goes on to the machining stage. The decision of how many to produce in a single batch is a function of the order pattern and the operational capacity. Batch production infers a degree of specialisation of both labour and plant. Some flexibility of operation is still necessary since a range of different products is still being produced. The specialisation and flexibility required is, however, less than that with jobbing.

Flow production can be used where there is a regular and consistent demand for a product such that the item can be produced for stock. The term *line* is sometimes used for this form of production since a production line is used. Workers, plant and tools can be geared to a single task which can then be constantly repeated. Each item thus starts at one end of the line and progresses along it, a particular task being carried out at each station. The car assembly line is an obvious example of such a form of production. For continuity of operation there has to be product standardisation and synchronisation (the term used is *balancing*) of each of the operations along the line to ensure that the output at each station matches that of the one preceding and the one following. With this form of production, breakdowns of machines can cause considerable disruption to the flow of work along the line. Thus, to avoid the entire line coming to a halt preventative maintenance is generally undertaken, rather than breakdown maintenance which might be acceptable with jobbing or even batch working. Preventative maintenance involves anticipating failure and replacing or adjusting the item concerned before failure occurs.

The *process* type of production involves materials being involved in a continuous process, the materials being transferred automatically from one part of the process to the next. An example of such a form of production is in the manufacture of chemicals or materials, where there is a continuous mixing and processing of the raw ingredients and a continuous production of the finished item. Such processes are designed to run continuously, all day and every day, and the workforce is mainly used in a monitoring capacity.

Table 3.1   Forms of production

Product capability	Type of production				
	Project	*Jobbing*	*Batch*	*Flow*	*Process*
Product range	Diverse ————————————————————→				Standard
Order size	One-off ————————————————→				Large
Make to order	Yes	Yes	Possibly	No	No
Make for stock	No	No	Possibly	Yes	Yes
Product standardisation	No	No	Some	Yes	Yes

Table 3.1 summarises the relationship between the type of production and the type of product required.

3.3 Implications of type of production

The type of production used is a consequence of the type of product required and has implications for plant layout, process planning, skills required of the workforce, production control, investment, costs and the type of organisation required. Thus, for example, jobbing requires high flexibility of plant and workers while flow production requires little. This is because with jobbing the tasks required are likely to vary from day to day as the product changes, while with flow production the plant is locked into a prescribed sequence of operations since the product is constant. Capital investment tends to be high with flow production since the production line involves a sequence of machines, each with a specific task. Jobbing to tackle a unique version of the same product might be feasible with such a single machine which is adjusted between the various operations. The degree of planning and control required with flow production is much higher than that required with jobbing. In jobbing the flexibility of the plant and labour means that changes can readily be accommodated, but, in flow production, changes are difficult to implement once the line has been established. The type of organisation involved with jobbing is inevitably decentralised since the workers have to be able to use their own initiative to adapt to changing requirements from one product to another. With flow production centralised organisation is essential since all aspects of the production are intimately geared to each other.

Table 3.2 summarises these implications. It is possible to find in some companies different forms of production being used for different

Table 3.2 Implications of forms of production

	Type of production				
Production implication	Project	Jobbing	Batch	Flow	Process
Flexibility of plant	High ←————————————— Low
Specialisation of plant	Low —————————————→ High
Plant utilisation	Low —————————————→ High
Specialisation of labour	Low —————————————→ High
Skills of labour	High ←————————————— Low
Methods standardisation	Low —————————————→ High
Capital investment	Low/high	Low————————————→ High
Cost/unit	High ←————————————— Low
Degree of planning	High	Low————————————→ High
Degree of control	High	Low————————————→ High
Organisation sells	Capability ——————————→ Product
Type of organisation	Decentralised ——————————→ Centralised

parts of a product. For example, batch production might be used for the production of some components while flow production is used for the assembly of the parts into the final product.

3.3.1 Plant layout

The plant layout is markedly affected by the type of production involved. The objectives involved in designing a plant layout include the need to reduce the total manufacturing time, reduce distances travelled by work-in-progress, ensure high utilisation of all the plant and ensure safe operation. There are three basic forms of layout:

1 Process
2 Product
3 Group.

With a *process* form of layout, all the plant associated with a particular type of process are grouped together. This is illustrated in Figure 3.2(a), which indicates the type of route that could be followed by an item requiring lathe work, drilling and milling in that sequence. This type of layout is characteristic of jobbing and batch types of production where the processes required can vary quite significantly from day to day, depending on the job concerned.

With *product* layout the plant is laid out according to the sequence of processes required by the product, as illustrated in Figure 3.2(b). This form of layout occurs with flow and process forms of production. The system is inflexible in that design or product changes may require the complete redesign of the line. The main benefits of this type of layout, when compared with a process layout, are:

1 reduced time spent by in-process components in transit between machines
2 reduced material handling
3 reduced operator expertise required
4 simpler production control procedures.

The disadvantages can include:

1 reduced machine shop flexibility
2 reduced job satisfaction.

For batch production the process form of layout can waste a lot of time with workpieces in transit between machines. In such situations a *group* layout may be used. Group layout involves the recognition that many of the products handled will have similarities in their make-up. Products are thus grouped into families, each member of a family being similar to the other members of the same family in the types of processes required. Plant may then be grouped to deal with the characteristics of a particular family. Thus, when a batch of products is required, the optimum use of the plant is achieved by the routeing of the work to that group of plant which has been set up to deal with the

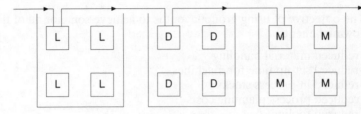

(a)

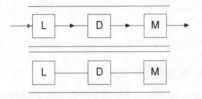

(b)

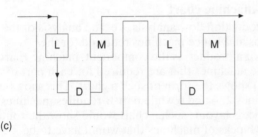

(c)

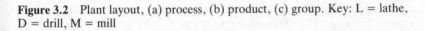

Figure 3.2 Plant layout, (a) process, (b) product, (c) group. Key: L = lathe, D = drill, M = mill

characteristics of the family in which the product is located. Within each group of machines, there is essentially a product layout with the work flowing between machines. Figure 3.2(c) illustrates this for a group requiring lathe work, drilling and milling. The maximum benefits of group layout can only be achieved if all the operations of a job are assigned to just one group of machines and not split between different groups.

The term *cellular* layout is sometimes used, with the term *group technology* being used to describe the grouping of components into families and the forming of groups of machines to manufacture families. Group layout requires that products be grouped according to their characteristics such as shape, size, form and material, i.e. their attributes. Coding methods have thus been developed which enable parts to be designated in such a way that commonalities can be readily determined (see Chapter 4 for a discussion of one method).

The objective of using group layout is to achieve some or all of the following benefits:

1 reduced material handling
2 reduced set-up time for machines
3 reduced in-process stocks
4 reduced process planning costs
5 reduced tooling costs
6 simpler production control procedures
7 greater job satisfaction.

Disadvantages include:

1 reduced machine shop flexibility
2 reduced machine utilisation
3 possibly increased job flow times.

However, the biggest problem is likely to be the cost and effort needed to change to a group layout.

3.3.2 Component–machine chart

One of the tools of production flow analysis, i.e. the analysis of the sequence of operations and hence machines required for the manufacture of parts of a product, is the component–machine chart. Such a chart shows the machines that are required for each part of a product. Figure 3.3(a) shows the form of such a chart. This shows that part A requires machines 2, 4 and 6 while part B requires machines 1, 4, 6 and 8. With a process layout, such a chart would show the routes between the different blocks of machines that would have to be followed by each part. With a product form of layout the chart would assist in planning the sequence of machines that would be needed. For group layout, parts with similar operations can be grouped together to give the revised form of the chart in Figure 3.3(b) and so indicate the forms of groups that could be used.

3.3.3 Automatic production

Automatic production involves three main aspects: machines which automatically perform operations; machines which automatically move materials from one machine to another; and control systems that regulate the performance of both the production and handling systems.

Automatic machines can be traced back to the early 1800s. A notable example was the machinery devised for the British Admiralty by Marc Brunel to manufacture pulley-blocks. From an input to the machine of timber, there emerged completed pulley blocks, the entire operation enabling 10 men to replace the 110 men that had previously been required to make 130 000 pulley-blocks per year. The pulley-block machine did not have automatic work transfer linking its various parts, hence the need for some men. A major advance was the automatic transfer machine, which could be described as a number of

Part

Machine	A	B	C	D	E	F	G	H	I	J	K
1		1			1					1	
2	1		1				1				
3				1		1			1		
4	1	1					1	1		1	1
5											
6	1	1	1		1			1		1	1
7		1									1
8		1			1			1		1	
9				1							
10				1		1			1		

(a)

Part

Machine	B	E	H	J	A	C	G	K	D	F	I	
1	1	1		1								⎫
4	1		1	1								⎬ Group I
6	1	1	1	1								
8	1	1	1	1								⎭
2					1	1	1					⎫
4					1		1	1				⎬ Group II
6					1	1	1					
7					1	1						⎭
3									1	1	1	⎫
9									1			⎬ Group III
10									1	1	1	⎭

(b)

Figure 3.3 Component–machine chart

machine stations mounted in sequence with workpieces being automatically moved between machines and fed in proper orientation to machines. Such a type of machine was probably first used by the Waltham Watch Company in 1888, and first applied in the car industry at Morris Motors in England about 1924 for the production of engines. Such types of machines became commonplace in the car industry and in many other industries involved in mass production in the 1930s. A major advance in automation was the advent of numerical control in the early 1950s. Successive positions of tools, machine tables, speeds and feed rates were indicated by the punch holes on a punched paper tape. The first computer-controlled systems appeared about 1959, with a computer being used to control chemical processing in the Texaco refinery at Port Arthur in Texas. Since then, many continuous processes, such as steel rolling mills and chemical processes, have been put under computer control. The extension of computer control to the manufacture of discrete components was slower in developing. The year 1960 saw the use of the first industrial installation of a robot, which was used to unload a die-casting machine at the General Motors car factory in New Jersey. In the 1970s the integration of automatic machines, automatic handling of material and computer control became established and the term computer-aided manufacturing (CAM) is now used. The 1980s saw the advent of flexible manufacturing systems (FMS) where a number of products could be made with a set of machines by the automatic control of those machines and the automatic movement of workpieces through the use of differing sequences. Thus flexible manufacturing systems enabled automation to be used with batches of components, where previously it had been largely restricted to flow production.

Computer-aided design (CAD) can be considered to have evolved in the 1960s, such a process giving both drafting and enabling analysis and manipulation of the resulting graphics. The integration of CAD and CAM has enabled computer-integrated manufacturing (CIM). This can incorporate computer-aided engineering, operations management, computer-aided manufacturing, computer-aided assembly, inspection and testing, and computer-controlled warehousing. Computer-aided engineering involves CAD, programming of numerical control tools, tool design and process planning. Operations management involves such items as production planning and control, cost accounting, and purchasing. Figure 3.4 outlines a possible structure for CIM.

Problems

Revision questions
1 List the main responsibilities that might be expected of a production manager.
2 Explain the different forms of production: project, jobbing, batch, flow and process.

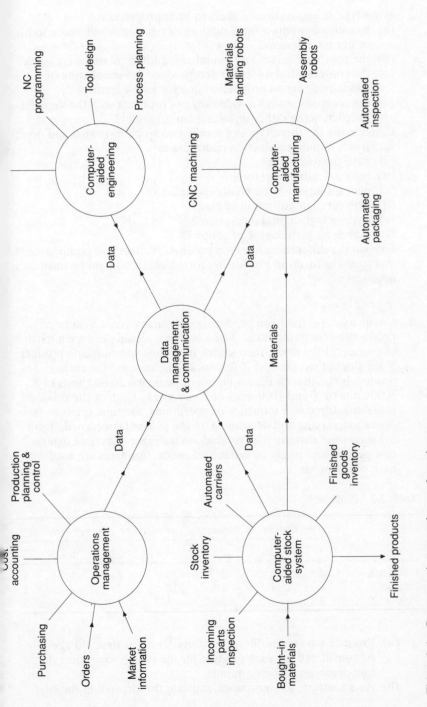

Figure 3.4 Computer-integrated manufacturing

3 What type of production is likely to be appropriate if
  (a) a customer wants a small number of items specially made to his or her own designs?
  (b) the company makes large numbers of identical items for stock?
  (c) the company has its tender accepted for the installation of a specially designed production line for a new factory?
  (d) the company makes a wide range of products with the demand for each being rather uncertain and irregular?
4 Considering the three types of production, jobbing, batch and flow, which will require production managers to
  (a) have flexible plant?
  (b) have a flexible workforce?
  (c) plan for labour to be highly specialised?
  (d) plan for high utilisation of plant?
  (e) require high capital investment?
  (f) exercise a high degree of control?
5 Explain the differences between process, product and group layout and state the forms of production for which each might be most appropriate.

Case problems

6 Company XYZ has been producing over many years a range of products by batch methods. The workforce would produce a batch of product X for stock, then switch for a time to producing product Y for stock, then product Z for stock. The demand for each product is stable with the requirement being for 20 000 units of X, 3000 units of Y and 1000 units of Z per week. Each of the products is manufactured in a sequence of operations, the time spent at each operation varying and depending on the product concerned. Table 3.3 shows the pattern. The production manager considers that the cost per product might be reduced if production lines are used for each of the products.

Table 3.3 Problem 6

	Output, in thousands, per machine type per week						
	1	2	3	4	5	6	7
Product X	5	4	2	10	2	1	5
Product Y	6	1	1	18			1
Product Z	1		1	4	1		5

  (a) Produce a paper outlining the considerations that will need to be considered for each product for the switch to production line operation to be economic.
  (b) As a footnote to your paper, indicate the changes in the

functions of the production manager that would be likely to occur if the change to production lines was made.

(c) The existing plant layout has similar machines grouped together. How would this have to change if production lines were adopted?

(d) Before the decision is made, the sales manager states that he thinks product Z will be superseded soon and a new design will be required. How easily could this change be accommodated if the production (i) remains as batch, (ii) has changed to line?

4 The product

4.1 Specification

Information about the content of each product and the standards of quality to be met in production are likely to be supplied as:

1 parts lists for each product and sub-assembly
2 purchasing specifications of the materials
3 drawings of each component with the tolerances and quality requirements included
4 assembly drawings
5 technical specifications of processing such as heat treatment.

Such information will be used by many sections in an organisation. For example, those responsible for ordering materials will use it to determine the form and quantity of materials required. Those responsible for process planning will use it to enable the sequence of operations to be planned, the tool requirements to be determined, etc. The quality control section will use it to check that specified standards are met. Production supervisors will use it to ensure that production proceeds in accordance with the required standards.

4.1.1 Part coding

A number of methods are used to code the parts that constitute a product. These include:

1 sequential coding
2 product coding
3 design coding.

With *sequential coding*, each drawing for a new part is coded sequentially. No form of classification is used, the resulting part number just indicating the sequence in which the drawings were made.

With *product coding* the parts are coded so as to indicate the product for which the parts were designed. Thus there may be an alphabetical code which indicates the product and a number which indicates the part for that product, e.g. ABC-123 would indicate a product coded ABC and part 123 for that product. In some case where there are sub-assemblies there may be a number of sections to the code, e.g. ABC-81-123 to indicate a product coded ABC, sub-assembly 81 with part 123 in that sub-assembly. With this form of coding the same part when used in different products will have different part numbers and there will be no easy means of identifying that the numbers refer to the same item.

With *design coding* the code has all parts for all products coded according to some general code. The same part will have the same code, regardless of which product it is used in. Such codes tend to have letters or digits indicating the nature and principal characteristics of a part. The code used may be a set of numbers which are hierarchical. Thus, for example, we may have R123B, where R indicates that the part is one which rotates, 1 that is round with some deviations, 2 that it is a gear, 3 that it is an external gear, and B that it is a bevel gear. With such a coding the significance to be attached to any one digit or letter depends on that preceding it. Thus, for example, the 1 in S123B would indicate something quite different to the 1 in R123B. An alternative form of design code is where each number independently indicates an attribute of the product. Such a form of coding is used in the Opitz method. For example, 101101520 with the Opitz code means

1 a round part with a length to diameter ratio less than 3 and greater than 0.5
0 a single outside diameter with no threads
1 a single internal diameter or stepped to one end without threads
1 planar machining of faces but no slots or grooves
0 no auxiliary holes or gear teeth
1 the outside diameter range
5 the material type and heat treatment
2 the initial material form
0 the tolerance grade.

The *Opitz code system* arose from the work of H. Opitz at Aachen University in Germany. He was investigating the requirements of the machine tools needed to produce parts used by industry in Germany. In doing this he found the need to devise a coding system to identify components. It is the development of this system which is now referred to as the Opitz system (see Opitz, H., *A Classification System to Describe Workpieces*, Pergamon Press, 1970). The basic code consists of a block of five digits detailing the form of the item followed by a block of four digits detailing information about the material. Each digit in each block represents a specific attribute:

First block

1st digit – whether the part is rotational or not and information about such factors as length to diameter ratio, with or without deviations
2nd digit – the external shape of the part
3rd digit – the internal shape of the part
4th digit – machining of plane surfaces
5th digit – additional holes, teeth and forming.

Second block

1st digit – dimensions
2nd digit – materials
3rd digit – original shape of raw material
4th digit – accuracy.

Design codes give classifications of parts and as such are useful in enabling greater standardisation, reducing the variety of parts, and in group technology where the layout of machines is determined by the characteristics of the parts (see section 3.3.1).

4.2 Development of process plans

The development of process plans is likely to go through a number of stages before the initial designs become implemented by manufacturing. In general terms, product planning is followed by process planning.

Product planning

1 The requirements for the product are assessed.
2 Taking into account the sales forecasts, decisions are made regarding the minimum possible costs. These have an impact on the design.
3 Drawing and specifications are evolved.

Process planning

4 The product is analysed into sub-assemblies and component parts. Assembly sequences are planned and assembly charts evolved which indicate the planned sequences.
5 Make or buy decisions are made with regard to component parts.
6 For those parts that are to be made in-company, decisions are made with regard to the processes.

7   If it is a major new development there may need to be
    consideration as to whether the processes are to be jobbing, batch
    or flow.
8   As a consequence there may need to be workplace and tool
    designs.
9   Specifications of how to manufacture the product are made and
    detailed in route sheets and operation sheets.

4.2.1   Make or buy?

Decisions on whether to make or buy an item will be determined by a
number of considerations. The following are some of the issues likely
to be involved:

1   Is the organisation able to make the item to the required quality
    and in the required volume at the required time?
2   Will there be a high degree of dependence on the availability of the
    item?
3   Are there suppliers who are suitable for the quality, volume and
    times required?
4   How does the cost of making the item compare with that of buying-
    in?
5   Would making the item give greater existing plant and employee
    utilisation, e.g. ironing out slack periods?

4.3   Variety control

Within an organisation the term *variety* can be applied to the variety of
products and services, the variety of parts in a product, the variety of
materials used, the variety of processes and the variety of skills
required by the employees. As variety increases so will organisation
problems, controllability and costs. For example, consider the
problems associated with the materials and bought-in components that
need to be stocked by an organisation. The greater the variety of
materials the greater will be the storage space required, the greater
will be the time spent in ordering, the greater the problems of keeping
track of the stock, etc. Variety control is thus vital. The aim of variety
control is to keep variety to a minimum.

   Variety control can result from simplification, standardisation and
specialisation. The term *simplification* is used to describe the reduction
of unnecessary variety, the term *standardisation* describes the control
of necessary variety. Thus standardisation means using, as far as is
possible, standard components and materials without resorting to
special components or materials. *Specialisation* means that an
organisation concentrates its effort on a limited range of products.

   Henry Ford is reputed to have said, 'You can have any colour of car
you like as long as it is black.' He had taken variety control to an
extreme, standardising on all aspects of the car, parts, shape and
colour. Customer choice can be reduced by variety control; however,

Ford was able to mass produce cars and as a consequence effect great economies and produce a cheap car. Some of the benefits of variety reduction can, however, be achieved by using standard parts without making the entire product standard. With modern cars, a small range of a particular model is produced using standard parts. Thus there are the standard and deluxe versions and different engine size models. Cost benefits can be maximised by concentrating on using those standard parts that have the highest tooling costs. This means standardising the shape of the bodywork but changing the colour of a production run is a simple matter to do.

The benefits of variety reduction include:

1 savings in design costs with fewer parts to design
2 less variety of bought-in components and materials means cost savings on storage space and stock control
3 larger quantities can be ordered of standard components and materials and lower prices may be obtained
4 use of standard parts means that production runs for those parts can be longer
5 production of standard items in long production runs means that production setting-up costs are minimised
6 production control is made simpler with fewer items and standard items
7 fewer products to market means there can be an intensification of selling effort
8 after-sales service can be better with fewer products to service.

4.3.1 Income and contribution ranking

Variety reduction for products means reducing the number of products offered. A basis on which the decision can be made with regard to which products to retain is the income and contribution generated by each. The *income* is the product of the number of items sold and the selling price. The *contribution* is the selling price minus the labour and material costs. The costs of overheads, such as that of running the plant, or paying for it, etc., are not considered. Thus, for example, we might have

Product A: income £1000, contribution £120
Product B: income £800, contribution £250
Product C: income £600, contribution £150
Product D: income £400, contribution −£50
Product E: income £350, contribution   £50

Ranked in order of income the products are A, B, C, D, E while ranked in order of contribution they are B, C, A, E, D. The minus sign for the contribution of D indicates a loss.

One possible strategy for variety reduction is to consider all those products for which the income is low, below perhaps a certain amount.

There may be reasons for the low income, e.g. the product has just been introduced and the sales have not yet reached their anticipated levels. The question that has to be considered with low-income products is whether the effort of producing them is worth while. Another possible strategy is to consider for variety reduction all those products for which the contribution is low, below perhaps a certain amount. Can the organisation afford to keep producing them when they contribute so little to the overhead costs and profit?

Another possible strategy, which takes into account both the income and the contribution, is to plot a contribution rank–income rank graph. The rank data for the products is shown in Table 4.1, with Figure 4.1 showing the graph. The dotted line on the graph is the line for which the contribution rank and order rank correspond. Points lying above this line need to be considered for possible cost reductions or increased selling prices in order to move them closer to the dotted line, i.e. they need to make a bigger contribution. Points lying below the line need to be considered for increases in sales volume in order to move them closer to the line, i.e. they need to produce a bigger income. If products cannot be moved closer to the dotted line then they need to be considered for possible elimination.

Table 4.1 Contribution rank–income rank data

Part	Income (£)	Income rank	Contribution (£)	Contribution rank
A	1000	1	120	3
B	800	2	250	1
C	600	3	150	2
D	400	4	−50	5
E	350	5	50	4

4.3.2 Pareto distribution

Another way the income–contribution data for products can be considered is by means of the *Pareto distribution*. This considers the percentage of the total income or contribution given by products. The procedure is:

1 Determine the total income generated by all the products. Thus, taking the income data given in section 4.3.1, total income is £3150.
2 Put the products in rank order and determine the accumulated income produced by successive products. Table 4.2 shows the result of doing this.
3 Calculate the percentage of the total income generated by the cumulative totals. This then shows the percentage of the total income generated by successive products in the income ranking list.

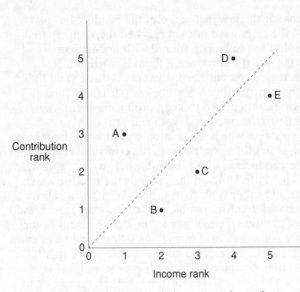

Figure 4.1 Contribution rank–income rank graph

The results given in Table 4.2 are generally drawn as a graph of
percentage income against percentage of range of products (Figure
4.2). Since there are five products, 20 per cent of the range generates
31.7 per cent of the income, 40 per cent of the range generates 55.4
per cent of the income, etc. The graph is often divided into three
sections, A, B and C. What the graph shows is that frequently a large
percentage of an organisation's income is generated by a relatively
small percentage of its products. An 80/20 relationship is often found,
i.e. 80 per cent of the income being generated by 20 per cent of the
products. Section A is then often taken as that percentage of the
products which generates 80 per cent of the income, B is that
percentage delivering up to 93 per cent of the income and C is that
delivering the final 7 per cent of the income. For this reason the graph
is sometimes called an *ABC graph*.

Table 4.2 Income distribution

Product	Income (£)	Income rank	Cumulative income (£)	% of total income
A	1000	1	1000	31.7
B	800	2	1800	55.4
C	600	3	2400	73.8
D	400	4	2800	86.1
E	350	5	3150	100

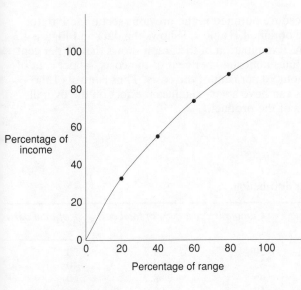

Figure 4.2 Pareto graph

Examination of such a graph enables consideration to be given as to whether some of the low-income products should be discontinued, since they contribute only a small percentage of the income. A similar graph can be used for the contribution of products.

This method of analysis is also used for the production control of batches to determine which batches should be given the greatest amount of control since they determine the greatest percentage of the workload; for the control of material or bought-in components to determine which should be given the most control since they determine the greatest percentage of the spending of the organisation; and for quality control to determine which types of defect causes the greatest percentage of defective components. The use of the method to determine which parts in a product are responsible for the greatest percentage of the costs is considered below.

4.4 Part costs

Consider the way the costs of parts of a product are distributed among those parts. For example, suppose there are five parts:

Part A, cost £20
Part B, cost £15
Part C, cost £10
Part D, cost £5
Part E, cost £1

40

Following the procedure outlined in the previous section, a Pareto distribution can be obtained. Table 4.3 shows the data and Figure 4.3 the resulting graph. Examination of the graph shows that 20 per cent of the parts constitutes almost 40 per cent of the costs, 40 per cent of the parts giving about 70 per cent of the costs. Thus control of the costs of these parts can have a very significant effect on the overall control of the costs of the product.

Table 4.3 Part costs distribution

Part	Cost (£)	Cost rank	Cumulative cost (£)	% of total cost	% of total parts
A	20	1	20	39.2	20
B	15	2	35	68.6	40
C	10	3	45	88.2	60
D	5	4	50	98.0	80
E	1	5	51	100	100

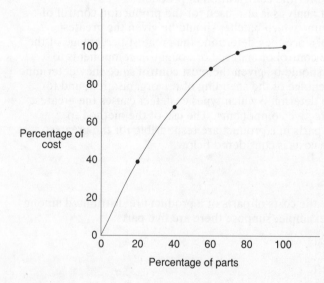

Figure 4.3 Distribution of costs of parts

4.5 Product life-cycle

Because of changes in technology, innovations by competitors, changes in costs, market saturation, etc., products in their original unmodified form tend to have a finite life span. The sales pattern of such a product tends to follow a life-cycle of the form shown in Figure 4.4. There are four general stages:

1 *Development stage* when the product is in its infancy and there is limited production to test the market. Teething problems are being remedied. Some products may not get beyond this stage.
2 *Growth stage* when the product has been accepted by the market and sales are rising.
3 *Maturity stage* when, perhaps, market saturation has occurred or competitors have brought out newer products or technological changes have overtaken the product. This could be the time to introduce a design improvement with the aim of extending the life of the product.
4 *Decline stage* when sales decline rapidly and the decision has to be made to stop making the product.

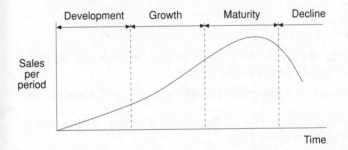

Figure 4.4 The product life-cycle

4.6 Value analysis

Value analysis is used to describe an organised and systematic way of determining how the required performance can be obtained at the lowest cost without affecting quality. The term *value analysis* is often used when an existing product is considered and the analysis is directed to considering if changes in the design of the product can reduce costs, the term *value engineering* being used when a new product is considered with the aim being to establish the lowest cost design.

Value analysis is concerned with considering the value of a product and how the costs associated with the product meeting the required purpose can be kept a minimum. There are two aspects to value, the value to the purchaser of the product carrying out the functions for which it was bought and the esteem value, i.e. the value associated with the status of owning the product.

Different authors have identified different numbers of steps in the process of carrying out value analysis. All, however, can be considered to involve the following broad steps:

1 *Function* Identify the function or functions required of the product and its parts.
2 *Alternatives* Consider all the possible ways of achieving these functions. This will mean considering such factors as number of parts, size, thickness of material, type of material, production methods, amount of waste material in processing, use of standard materials and parts, whether to buy-in or make in-company, suppliers, quantities involved, etc.
3 *Costs* Ascertain the costs of the various alternatives.
4 *Evaluation* Evaluate the costed alternatives and determine the optimum one.

The approach can be paraphrased in the following questions:

1 What is it required to do?
2 What else will do it?
3 What will it cost?
4 Which is the best approach?

To illustrate the above, consider the redesign of a mains electric plug. The functions required of the plug are that:

1 it conforms to the appropriate standards (e.g. British standard BS 1363)
2 it enables connection to be made between a cable and the mains electric supply via a fused link.

The conventional design is that of a two-part plastic moulding into which the various component parts slot or screw. These parts are the three pins which make electrical contact with the mains cable. The neutral and earth wires in the cable are connected directly to two of the pins. The live wire, has to make connection to its pin via a mounting which can hold a fuse. The cable entering the plug has to be restrained from movement, usually by two screws clamping a flexible strip across it. There is also a screw which is used to hold the two parts of the plug together and enable it to be opened for fuse changing. Figure 4.5 shows the detail of such a plug. In considering alternatives the questions that might be posed are: Does the casing have to be in two parts? Does the plug have to be separated into two pieces for the fuse to be changed? Could the number of parts in the plug be reduced and so simplify assembly? Could the cable clamp be by some other means and so reduce the need for screws? Is there any other possible means of linking wires and pins so that screws can be avoided? Can the wiring of a plug by a customer be made simpler? In looking at the existing design, a Pareto analysis might be made to find out which parts contribute most to the costs and, therefore, which parts are most capable of having significant effect on the overall product cost and are worth considering in most detail. In the case of the plug, this might be the labour costs involved in assembling the plug; hence attention can be focused on the number of parts to be assembled and the methods used to assemble them.

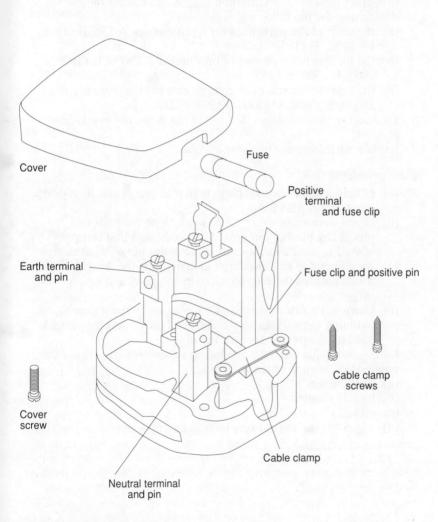

Cover

Fuse

Positive terminal and fuse clip

Earth terminal and pin

Fuse clip and positive pin

Cable clamp screws

Cover screw

Cable clamp

Neutral terminal and pin

Figure 4.5   Mains electric plug

44

Problems

Revision questions

1 Explain the principles involved in the different types of part coding.
2 Explain what is meant by *control of variety* and indicate some of the benefits that can occur from it being practised in an organisation.
3 Explain the difference between *simplification* and *standardisation*.
4 Explain how a Pareto distribution can be obtained and explain two of its uses.
5 Construct the Pareto distribution graphs and discuss their significance for the following situations:
   (a) the costs of the parts used for a product are A £30, B £10, C £4, D £2, E £1;
   (b) the income from a range of products is A £6000, B £1000, C £800, D £300, E £100;
   (c) the costs of the stocks of components held in store are A £5000, B £3000, C £500, D £300, E £100.
6 Explain the various stages that can occur in the life of a typical product.
7 Explain what is meant by *value analysis*.

Case problems

8 (a) Obtain a mains electric plug, take it to pieces and then devise an assembly plan for it.
   (b) If you were employed by a company with facilities for processing plastics but none for metals, and that company wished to use its facilities to make mains plugs, what factors would need to be considered in arriving at the decisions as to which parts of the plug to make in-company and which to buy-in?
   (c) Carry out a value analysis of the plug and write a paper outlining the various possibilities and the effects they might have on the overall costs of the plug.
9 Carry out a value analysis, producing a paper which outlines the possibilities, on one of the following:
   (a) car bumpers
   (b) bicycle pumps
   (c) bicycles
   (d) chairs for use in company or college canteens.

5 Quality control

5.1 Quality

In everyday language the term *quality* tends to mean a Rolls-Royce rather than a cheap car. However, in terms of fitness for purpose, a cheap car might fit perfectly the requirements of a student whereas a Rolls-Royce would not. In technical language the term 'quality' is used to mean that a product is one which is fit for its purpose or meets requirements. The standard definition of quality is: *Quality is the totality of features and characteristics of a product or service that bear on its ability to meet stated or implied needs* (BS 4778: Part 1: 1987; ISO 8402–1986: Quality vocabulary).

The quality of the products and services offered by an organisation is an important concern to both the organisation and its customers. Customers' confidence in the quality of the products and services is an important factor in determining the demand for the organisation's products and services. An organisation needs to deliver, to the customers, products and services which are to the customers' requirements or fit for the purposes for which they were bought. The quality of products is also important to the manufacturer since quality deficiencies can result in additional costs arising from reworking, increased scrap, and the handling of complaints.

Quality and reliability are related, with reliability being a consequence of quality. The term *reliability* in relation to a product is defined as being the ability of the product to function as required, when and where required, and for the time required.

5.2 Standards for quality systems

The standards for a quality system are laid out in the British Standard BS 5750 and in an identical way in Euro Norm EN 29000 and International Standards Organisation ISO 9000.

BS 5750: Part 0: Section 0.1 (EN 29000, ISO 9000)   This is a general introduction to the selection of quality systems, the standards available and their use.

BS 5750: Part 1 (EN 29001, ISO 9001)   This is the specification for use when the organisation is involved in the design/development of products, as well as production, installation and servicing. The quality of the products from the organisation involve a consideration of design/development, production, installation and servicing.

BS 5750: Part 2 (EN 29002, ISO 9002)   This is the specification for organisations concerned only with the production and installation of products to an established design.

BS 5750: Part 3 (EN 29003, ISO 9003)   This is the specification for use where the conformance of an organisation to contractual specifications is determined by its capabilities in just inspection and testing.

BS 5750: Part 0: Section 0.2 (EN 29004, ISO 9004)   This is a guide to quality management and quality system elements.

BS 5750: Part 4: 1990   This is a guide to the use of BS 5750: Parts 1, 2 and 3.

The part of the standard which is relevant to an organisation depends on its activities. If the organisation has a design function, then Part 1 is relevant. If the organisation has no design facility but manufactures or processes products to standard or customer designs, then Part 2 is relevant. If the organisation is only providing products which it has not made but is testing for quality, then Part 3 is relevant.

Organisations can be certified as conforming to the standard, such certification resulting from government accredited certification companies assessing the quality systems of the organisations. Once an organisation has been certified it is awarded a certificate and is subject to periodic reassessment to ensure that its performance is maintained.

5.2.1   Key points

The following paragraphs outline some of the key features of the standard. For more information the reader is referred to the actual standard or to some of the texts devoted to explaining the implementation of the standard (e.g. Holmes, K., *Implementing BS 5750*, PIRA International, 1991).

The organisation has to establish and maintain an effective system for ensuring that its products and services conform to the specified requirements of the customers. The standard requires the top management in an organisation to be committed to quality. They must produce a written quality policy and everyone in the organisation should know of the existence of the policy and its message. This policy is to indicate how management is going to manage quality and is likely to include such items as an understanding that quality means fitness for purpose and not grade of product, that the prevention of poor quality is more profitable than correction of defects after the event, and that every employee should make quality a way of work.

The policy is likely to be backed up by a quality plan to indicate clearly how the quality system is to work and how the requirement of the standard are to be met. Quality procedures have to be specified. Thus, responsibilities have to be allocated for every aspect of the quality system so that, for instance, it is clear who is able to stop production if quality is suspect. How quality is to be assured must also be established. This requires a specification of the checks to be used for products, how they are to be done, who is to do them and when. Management responsibility for quality requires that they allocate responsibility to an individual to see that the policy is implemented. They must also periodically review the system to ensure that it continues to meet requirements.

Providing quality products means providing products which meet the needs of the customers. This can only be achieved when the needs of the customers are known. The term *contract review* is used to describe the need to establish what the customers want. Checklists may be a useful way of ensuring that sales representatives obtain all the relevant information.

The contract review specifies what is required, and the next step is to ensure that all the materials and services purchased by the organisation are such as to enable the required quality of the final product to be obtained. This will be made easier if suppliers are also working to the standard, and so their contract review will mean that they are concerned with ensuring that what is supplied is what is required. However, there will still be a duty for the organisation to check that the purchased materials conform to requirements.

Products need to be coded so that at all stages of production it is possible to identify them. At a minimum, there should be a job number which follows a product through its various stages of manufacture. This means that it is possible to identify the processing history of a particular product, job or batch and so have traceability. Thus, for example, with a particular batch of products there may be a need to identify the machine that was used for drilling, the heat treatment batch that was used, etc. This also assists in establishing the possible cause of problems.

The standard's process control requirements are that those parts of the process that can affect quality must be identified and quality control plans established. These would include such information as the tests that should be made, how they should be made, and when. Thus, for example, with a machine stamping out parts from sheet metal there may be a requirement that every 15 minutes a batch of 10 is taken and measured, using a specified instrument, to ensure that the measurement lies within the prescribed limits. Any statistical techniques used to sample products need specification.

The accuracy to which inspection measurements are to be made has to be specified. The measurement and test equipment used in inspection must thus be selected to ensure that this accuracy can be obtained and the procedures for its use should be detailed. Calibration procedures need to be instituted with calibration records being maintained.

Inspection and testing includes the inspection of purchased materials, in-process inspection and final inspection. Thus, for example, in the stock control of incoming materials there may be a requirement that a tensile test specimen be cut from every batch of steel and that the results of such a test should lie within certain prescribed limits. Until the test is completed and the results accepted, the material is not accepted for use.

Final inspection means a check that the product has passed all the inspection and can be accepted as having attained the pass grade, there having to be criteria clearly laid down as to what constitutes a pass or a fail. There also needs to be a quality record which shows that each quality check has been signed off.

The standard requires that handling, storage, packing and delivery of products should have procedures specified so that quality is protected. Thus, for example, storage facilities for finished products should not be permitted to deteriorate: for, example, storage in damp conditions leading to rust problems.

The operation and maintenance of all quality control procedures has to be fully documented. Communication to the customer about the quality control procedures associated with a product is an essential part of quality assurance.

5.3 Quality-related costs

There are two distinct but interrelated aspects for the quality of a product, these being the product design quality and the product manufacture quality. The *product design quality* is a measure of how well the design specification of the product meets the customers' design requirements. The *product manufacture quality* is a measure of how well the product, after being manufactured, conforms to the design requirements.

There are two factors which will affect the quality requested by the customer: precision and reliability. If the customer is prepared to pay enough then a highly precise product with high reliability can be obtained. However, there is usually a trade-off of precision and reliability against cost in the required specification.

Figure 5.1 shows, in a general way, how the cost and value to the customer are likely to depend on the precision required in the manufacturing as a result of the design specification. Thus the higher the required precision, i.e. the tighter the tolerances, the greater will be the cost of a product, the cost rising at an ever-increasing rate as higher precision is specified. The value to the customer of precision is likely to decrease as higher precisions are considered. Thus there is likely to be an optimum precision when there is the maximum difference between the value and cost to the customer.

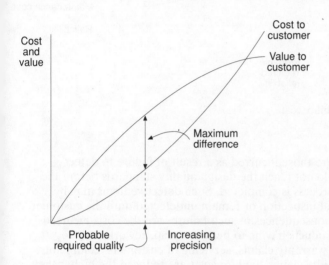

Figure 5.1　The cost and value of precision

Figure 5.2 shows, in a general way, how the cost of a product is likely to be related to reliability. A low-reliability product can be produced cheaply but is likely to incur high maintenance costs. Increasing the reliability decreases the maintenance costs. As the graph indicates, there is a balance between the initial cost of a product and the maintenance cost for which the total cost is a minimum. This is likely to be the required reliability.

5.3.1　The economics of quality
With a specified quality of design it is the task of manufacturing to produce products to this specification and hence to the quality required by the customer. The costs incurred in this can be grouped under the headings of failure costs, prevention costs and appraisal costs.

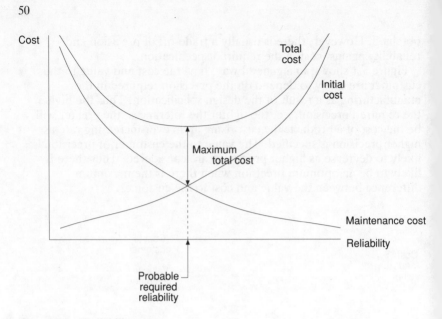

Figure 5.2 Reliability cost

Failure costs are those incurred as a result of failure to detect products which do not reach the design quality standards before the manufacturing process is completed. Such defective items may be detected at a final inspection or remain undetected until the customer uses them. The consequences of such failures are the costs incurred with defective products having to become scrap, rework costs to remedy defects, warranty claims, servicing of customers' complaints, and product liability claims. Failure costs are reduced the higher the amount of quality control exercised during the manufacture, as illustrated in Figure 5.3.

Prevention costs are the costs associated with the design, implementation and maintenance of a quality system. They are designed to prevent products reaching the end of the manufacturing process and not being of the required quality. The costs of quality system involve those incurred in the planning of the system, the creation and maintenance of it, inspection equipment, training of operators, supervisors and managers. The greater the amount of quality control exercised, the greater the cost (Figure 5.3).

Appraisal costs are involved in checking quality and ensuring that the quality system is functioning satisfactorily, i.e. quality audits. It thus includes such costs as those incurred in the inspection and testing of incoming materials, process set-ups, intermediate and final products. It also includes the costs of the calibration and maintenance of inspection equipment. As the effort placed on prevention increases

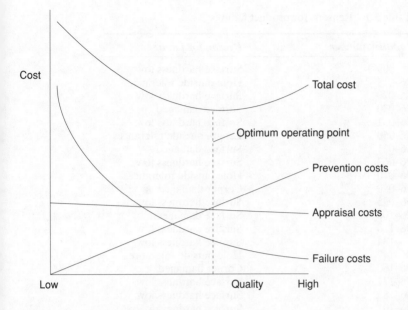

Figure 5.3 Costs of quality control

so the cost of appraisal diminishes, as illustrated in Figure 5.3.

The total cost of low quality to an organisation is predominantly due to failure costs. However, as more money is spent on prevention, the total cost reduces as the quality improves. An optimum operating point is reached when the total cost is at a minimum. Spending more money on prevention will result in higher quality but also higher total cost.

5.4   Where to inspect

Within the manufacturing process there are a number of possible points at which inspection can occur. The decisions as to where to inspect will depend on a number of factors, including the importance of a manufacturing stage in determining whether a product will be of the required quality, and the effect of the time spent on inspection of the flow of the product through the manufacturing processes.

5.4.1   Pareto analysis

The establishment of the main types of problems in the manufacturing of products can be aided by a Pareto analysis (see section 4.3.2). Thus it might be used to establish the main types of defects occurring and to determine where most effort needs to be expended to reduce failures.

Table 5.1 Reasons for product failures

Product number	Reason for failure
06–009	Surface hardness low
06–015	Hole outside tolerances
06–020	Surface hardness low
06–030	Surface damaged
06–031	Surface hardness low
06–050	Length outside tolerances
06–051	Surface damaged
06–063	Surface hardness low
06–070	Hole outside tolerances
06–080	Corner damaged
06–095	Surface hardness low
06–106	Surface damaged
06–120	Surface hardness low
06–134	Surface hardness low
06–147	Hole outside tolerances
06–160	Corner damaged
06–171	Surface hardness low
06–183	Surface hardness low
06–201	Surface hardness low
06–215	Hole outside tolerances

Table 5.2 Pareto analysis of Table 5.1

Type of defect	Frequency	Rank	Cumulative frequency	% of total frequency
Surface hardness low	10	1	10	50
Hole outside tolerances	4	2	14	70
Surface damaged	3	3	17	85
Corner damaged	2	4	19	95
Length outside tolerances	1	5	20	100

For example, consider the situation described by Table 5.1, which lists the reasons for products being rejected at a final inspection. From that table we can determine the number of times a particular form of defect occurs for the number of batches considered. The defects can then be put in rank order and the accumulated number obtained of defects occurring by successive defects in the rank list. This number can then be expressed as a percentage of the total number of defects. Table 5.2 shows that 50 per cent of the defects are caused by the surface hardness being low. This could indicate that attention should be directed at the heat treatment process. To avoid work proceeding unnecessarily on products which are going to be defective as a result of faulty heat treatment, an inspection immediately after heat treatment could be used. Better control of the heat treatment process might assist in preventing defects occurring.

5.5 Statistical quality control techniques

Statistical quality control techniques are concerned with answering the question of how the products should be inspected and the interpretation of the outcomes of such inspections. Samples are taken, and the inspection of the samples are used to determine the quality of entire batches or the functioning of some process. Thus, for example, the final manufactured product inspection may involve taking a sample of five items from a batch of 100 and, on the basis of that inspection, passing or rejecting the entire batch as not being to the required specification. It could also involve an inspection of a sample of, say, five items produced every hour from a particular machine and on the basis of that inspection determining whether the machine is operating to specification or requires some adjustment.

There are two main types of data that may be gathered by inspection. In some cases the inspection may be on the basis of whether an item is right or wrong, i.e. whether it fits the required specification or not. Such a form of inspection typically occurs as the final product inspection when a component is accepted for stock or despatch to a customer. In such cases the quality control is termed *control by attributes*. Where the product has some property that can vary, e.g. the diameter of a hole or the length of a component, then inspection as part of the process control may involve a measurement of the variable. This type of quality control is termed *control by variables*. Such control is typically of the inspection that occurs to monitor the performance of a particular machine and operator to check that they are functioning in the normal manner. The difference between these two forms of data is that, in one case, the data gathered is continuously variable while, in the other, it is has just two values, right or wrong.

The following sections in this chapter outline some of the issues and techniques involved in carrying out statistical quality control. For a more detailed account the reader is referred to specialist texts, e.g. Oakland, J.S., *Statistical Process Control*, Heinemann, 1986.

5.6 Acceptance sampling

Acceptance sampling is concerned with taking a sample from a batch and, on the basis of that sample, deciding whether to accept or reject the batch. It is sampling by attributes.

How big a sample needs to be taken so that the inspection data on the sample is typical of the batch as a whole? To illustrate this problem, consider a pack of playing cards. There are 52 cards in the pack, of which four are kings. Consider the kings to be the defective items in a batch of 52 items. Suppose we take a sample of four cards from the pack. What is the chance that our sample will include a king? What is the chance that the proportion of kings in the sample will mirror the proportion in the pack? The sample might have no kings and thus suggest that there are no kings in the pack. The sample might include four kings and suggest that if this pattern continued throughout the pack we would have a pack which was made up entirely of kings. However, the chance of drawing all four kings is fairly low. The problem is thus to choose a sample size which has a reasonable chance of representing the properties of the pack as a whole.

In the above discussion, and that which follows, the term *chance*, or *probability*, is used. With the pack of card there are four kings in a total of 52 cards. Thus, in taking one card from the pack there are 52 possible cards which can be drawn of which just four are kings. The term *chance*, or the term *probability*, is the number of ways a particular event can occur divided by the total number of possibilities. Thus the chance of drawing one card as a king is 4/52. This does not mean that every time you draw a single card from the pack that it will be a king, merely that if you repeatedly draw a single card from the pack then, in the long run, four times in every 52 it will be a king. The higher the chance of an event the more often it will occur. A chance of 1 means that it will happen every time; a chance of 0 that it will never happen.

5.6.1 Sampling plans

The term *acceptance quality level* (AQL) is used to define the highest percentage of rejects in a batch which the receiver of the goods will regularly accept. Tables are available to enable this to be translated into the maximum number of rejects that should occur in a sample taken from the batch for the batch to be accepted (see section 5.6.2 for a mathematical discussion of this point). For example, if the acceptance quality level is, say, 4 per cent then for a batch of 100 a sample of 13 should be taken and passed if there are no rejects, or only one, and failed if there are two or more. With the acceptance quality level of 4 per cent and a batch size of 50 then a sample of three should be taken and passed if there are no rejects and failed if there is one or more.

The above represents what is termed a *single sampling plan*, just one sample being taken from a batch, with the decision to accept it or reject it being based on the result of that inspection. There are other forms of sampling plans. With a *double sampling plan* a sample is taken and if the number of defective items is less than some number the batch is accepted, if greater than some number it is rejected. Thus, for example, with a sample of 100 the batch may be accepted when the number of defective items is two or less and rejected if the number of defective items is seven or more. If the number of defective items is between the acceptance and rejection levels, i.e. for the example greater than two and less than seven, then a second 100 sample is taken. The batch is accepted if the total number of defective items in the two samples is seven or less, otherwise it is rejected. With *multiple sampling plans* the procedure outlined for the double sampling plan is extended to cover multiple samples being taken.

The problem with taking samples is that rejection or acceptance of a batch is based on the chance that the sample taken is representative of the batch as a whole. The smaller the sample in relation to the batch size the greater the chance that it will not be representative. There is thus a chance that a batch will be rejected when the actual percentage of defective items in the batch is low enough for acceptance. The chance that this will occur is known as the *producer's risk* since it is the producer of the batch who is losing out. Conversely, there is a chance that a batch will be accepted when the actual percentage of defective items in the batch is high enough for rejection. This chance is known as the *consumer's risk* since it is the consumer receiving the batch who is losing out. The sampling plan used is thus a trade-off between the costs of the sampling and the risk that a batch will be wrongly rejected or accepted.

For example, if we had a batch of 100 items of which 10 per cent were defective, i.e. 10 in the batch of 100, then taking a sample of 10 we should ideally obtain one defective item in the sample, i.e. 10 per cent of the sample defective, if it was representative of the batch as a whole. However, just taking at random 10 items from a batch of 100 there is a 35 per cent chance that we will find samples with zero defective items. If the acceptable quality level for the batch was 5 per cent then there is a 35 per cent chance that the batch would be incorrectly accepted on the basis of a sampling plan which required us to find one defective item in a batch of 10 in order to reject the batch. This is the consumer's risk. With the sample there is a 39 per cent chance that we will find samples with one defective item. There is a 26 per cent chance that we will find samples with more than one defective item. Thus if the acceptable quality level for the batch was 10 per cent then, on the basis of the sampling plan whereby rejection occurs if there is more than one defective item in a sample, there is a 26 per cent chance that the batch would be incorrectly rejected. This is the producer's risk.

We can describe the consequences of a particular sampling plan by means of a graph called the *operating characteristic*. For example, suppose we have a sampling plan whereby a sample of 10 is taken from a batch and the batch is accepted when the sample contains 0, 1 or 2 defective items. With a sample of 10 the chance of finding 0, 1 or 2 defective items in the sample is 0.93 when the batch contains 10 per cent defective items, 0.68 when it contains 20 per cent defective items, 0.38 when it contains 30 per cent defective items and 0.17 when it contains 40 per cent. Figure 5.4 shows the operating characteristic, it being a graph of the chance that a batch will be accepted plotted against the percentage of defective items in the batch. The graph tells us the chance that the sampling plan will accept a batch containing particular percentages of defective items. For example, the graph indicates that there is a 50 per cent chance that a batch containing about 25 per cent defective items will be accepted. If we set the producer's risk as 10 per cent, then the graph indicates that the percentage of defectives in the batch that will be accepted, with this sampling plan, is up to about 12 per cent. If we set the consumer's risk as 10 per cent, then the graph indicates that the percentage of defectives in the batch that might be accepted is up to nearly 50 per cent.

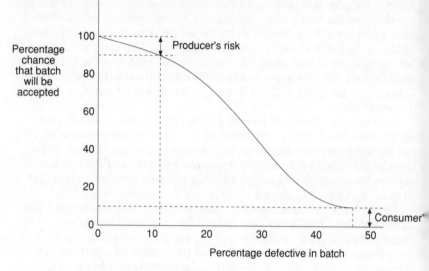

Figure 5.4 An operating characteristic

An operating characteristic which has a rapid fall from a high chance of a batch being accepted to a low chance is desirable since it gives a smaller region where there are reasonable chances that a batch with a particular number of defective items will in some cases be accepted and in others rejected. An operating characteristic can be made steeper by increasing the sample size but still rejecting the same proportion as defective, as illustrated in Figure 5.5.

5.6.2 The binomial expression

This section presents a mathematical derivation of the data quoted above. Consider a process which produces a product for which the proportion defective is p. For example, if p was 0.1 then for a batch of 100 we would have 10 defective products. The chance of taking one item from the batch and finding it to be defective is therefore p. The proportion of a batch which is acceptable is q. Thus if we have 90 acceptable items in a batch of 100 then q is 0.9. The proportion q is

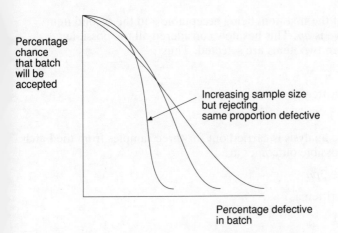

Figure 5.5 Effect of sample size on operating characteristic

just $(1 - p)$. The chance of taking one item from the batch and finding it to be acceptable is q. The chance of taking one item from the batch and finding it to be either acceptable or defective is 1, i.e. a certainty since there are no other possibilities.

$p + q = 1$

When two or more events are required to follow consecutively, then the probability of them all happening is the product of their individual probabilities. We can illustrate this with a simple example. The chance of a coin landing heads uppermost when dropped is 1/2, this being because there is just one way out of a possible two that such an event can happen. The two ways are either heads uppermost or tails uppermost. If we drop two coins then the ways they can land are:

first coin heads, second coin heads
first coin heads, second coin tails,
first coin tails, second coin heads,
first coin tails, second coin tails.

There is thus just one way in four that both will land heads uppermost. The chance of both being heads is thus 1/4. But a quarter is just a half multiplied by a half, i.e. the chance is just the product of the chances of heads for each coin.

If we now take two items from the batch then the chance of the first item being defective is p and the chance of the second item being defective is p. The chance of both items in the sample being defective is thus p^2. The chance of the first item being acceptable is q and the chance of the second item being acceptable is q. The chance of both items in the sample of two being acceptable is q^2. The chance of the first item being defective and the second item being acceptable is pq.

The chance of the first item being acceptable and the second item being defective is qp. This has now considered all the possible outcomes when two items are selected. Thus

$$p^2 + 2pq + q^2 = 1$$

This can be written as

$$(p + q)^2 = 1$$

If the above analysis is carried out for three samples from the batch, then all the possible outcomes are

$$p^3 + 3p^2q + 3pq^2 + q^3 = 1$$

This can be written as

$$(p + q)^3 = 1$$

In general, if we take a sample of n from a batch for which the proportion p is defective and q acceptable

$$(p + q)^n = 1$$

This is known as the *binomial expression*. The expansion of such an expression gives a sequence of terms, each of which gives the chances of certain combinations of events occurring within the sample. The expansion of the expression is

$$(p + q)^n = p^n q^0 + p^{n-1}q^2 + p^{n-2}q^3 + \ldots + p^0 q^n$$

Thus the term for finding x defectives in a sample size of n is

$$p^x q^{n-x} = p^x(1 - p)^{n-x}$$

Hence, for example, the chance of finding no defective items in a sample of 5 taken from a batch where the proportion defective is 0.1 is

$$0.1^0(1 - 0.1)^{5-0} = 0.59$$

The chance of finding one defective item in the sample is

$$0.1^1(1 - 0.1)^{5-1} = 0.066$$

The chance of finding two defective items in the sample is

$$0.1^2(1 - 0.1)^{5-2} = 0.0073$$

If the sampling plan was to accept if there was 0 or 1 defective item in the sample, then the chance of doing this is $0.59 + 0.066$ or about 0.66. If an event, i.e. acceptance, can happen in a number of alternative ways then the chance of the event occurring is the sum of the chances of the individual occurrences.

5.6.3 Control charts for attributes

Control charts are used to monitor how the number of defective items in samples changes with successive samples. Figure 5.6, on which

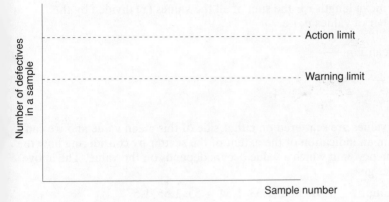

Figure 5.6 Control chart for attributes

action and warning limit lines are marked, shows such a chart. These lines are drawn for a particular sample size so that if the action limit is exceeded corrective action is required and if the warning limit is exceeded further samples should be taken to see if the trend continues and action is required. Typically the action limit is set so that there is only a 1 in 100 chance of its being exceeded when the products are being produced to the right quality. The warning limit is set to a 1 in 20 chance.

5.7 Process variations

If any of the variable characteristics of products are considered, random variations will be found. There is an inherent variability in every manufacturing process which results in products having characteristics which vary one from another in a random way. Thus if, after some process, the length of a number of products is measured then variations in length will be found. With products which are to the right quality this variation occurs within the tolerances permitted. Thus we might have, for example, 100.0 ± 0.1 mm, and with the random variation only resulting in variations within that tolerance, all the products are acceptable. This random variation may, however, be superimposed on some other change, e.g. a length change resulting from a faulty machine setting. The problem is then to devise procedures which enable the results due to a faulty setting to be recognised in the presence of random variations due to normal manufacturing variability.

Suppose the results of an inspection of the lengths of a batch of product show:

1.54, 1.53, 1.55, 1.57, 1.52, 1.54, 1.52, 1.54, 1.53, 1.54,
1.54, 1.56, 1.56, 1.54, 1.53, 1.51, 1.55, 1.54, 1.56, 1.53

The mean length $\bar{x}$ is the sum of all the values (x) divided by the number of values n, i.e.

$$\text{mean } \bar{x} = \frac{\Sigma x}{n}$$

$$= \frac{30.8}{20} = 1.54.$$

The values are scattered on either side of this mean value and we can obtain an indication of the extent of the scatter by considering how the frequency with which a value occurs depends on the value. The above values give

Value	1.51	1.52	1.53	1.54	1.55	1.56	1.57
Frequency	1	2	4	7	2	3	1

Figure 5.7 shows the above results plotted as a histogram.

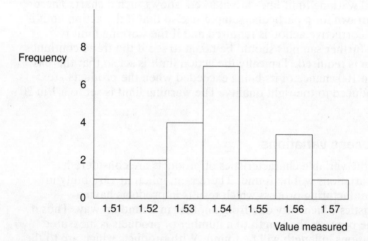

Figure 5.7 Distribution of values

With the steps in the histogram smoothed out to give a graph showing how the frequency with which a value occurs, then if only random causes are present the result tends to be of the form shown in Figure 5.8. Such a form of graph is referred to as a *normal distribution*. The distribution is symmetrical about the mean value and has a constant shape. To describe the spread of data about the mean value the term standard deviation, symbol σ, is used (see below for an explanation of the term): 68.3 per cent of the values will lie within one standard deviation of the mean; 95.4 per cent will lie within two standard deviations; and 99.7 per cent within three standard

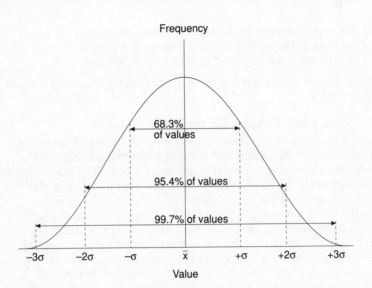

Figure 5.8 Normal distribution

deviations. The deviation for a particular value is the difference between the value x and the mean $\bar{x}$, e.g. 1.51 has a deviation of

Deviation $= x - \bar{x}$
$\qquad\quad = 1.51 - 1.54 = -0.03$

Values below the mean have a negative deviation; values above, a positive deviation. The sum of all the deviations will be zero, the negative values cancelling out the positive values. A measure of the average deviation that occurs is, however, given by finding the average of the squares of the deviations. The standard deviation σ of a set of data is then the square root of this average, i.e.

$$\sigma = \sqrt{\frac{\Sigma(x - \bar{x})}{n}}$$

with n being the number of items. With small numbers of items, the above equation gives an underestimate of the standard deviation and the following equation is used:

$$\sigma = \sqrt{\frac{\Sigma(x - \bar{x})}{n - 1}}$$

Thus, for example, if we have a process which is cutting lengths of metal to a value of 200 mm with a standard deviation of 5 mm then we can say that we should expect, if there are only random variations, that inspections give

68.3 per cent of the results within ±5 mm of 200 mm,
95.4 per cent of the results within ±10 mm of 200 mm,
99.7 per cent of the results within ±15 mm of 200 mm.

If there are more values outside these limits then the variation is more than just random.

5.7.1 Mean control charts for variables

Figure 5.9 shows the basic form of a *mean control chart*. A sample is taken, the variable measured and the mean determined. Thus, for example, the variable may be the diameter of a hole. The sample mean is then marked on the chart. The chart has two pairs of lines either side of the mean obtained for the product from a number of samples obtained when it is known that the process is operating satisfactorily. The lines 3.09σ from the mean are marked as the upper and lower action limits. The chance of the value falling outside this number of standard deviations from the mean purely as a result of random variations is 1 in 1000. Thus, if the value falls outside then action should be taken since there is a 1 in 1000 chance that it is required. The lines 1.96σ from the mean are marked as the lower and upper warning limits. The chance of the sample mean falling outside this number of standard deviations of the mean is 1 in 40. Thus if this happens then there is ground for suspicion that all may not be well and a further sample should be taken to see if it confirms the need for action.

The calculation of the control limits for a mean control chart is generally simplified by the use of tables.

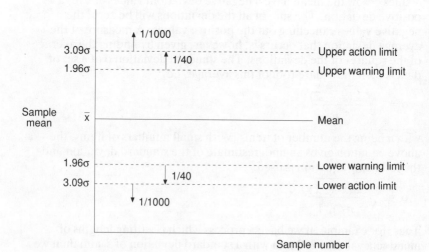

Figure 5.9   Mean control chart

Action limit $= \bar{x} \pm A'_{0.001}\bar{R}$

Warning limit $= \bar{x} \pm A'_{0.025}\bar{R}$

where $\bar{R}$ is the mean range occurring within a number of sets of samples, generally 10 or more, and $A'_{0.001}$ and $A'_{0.025}$ are constants that can be looked up in tables. Table 5.3 gives some values for different samples sizes. The values of these constants depend on the size of sample involved. For example, for a sample size of 5 then $A'_{0.001} = 0.59$ and $A'_{0.025} = 0.3$. Hence, if a sample gave values of

5.100, 5.102, 5.105, 5.101, 5.103

then its range is the difference between the maximum and minimum values, i.e. $5.105 - 5.100 = 0.005$. This procedure is repeated for, say, 10 sets of samples and the range determined for each. For example, the ranges might be

0.005, 0.004, 0.006, 0.007, 0.003,
0.006, 0.005, 0.004, 0.005, 0.005

The mean range is then $0.050/10 = 0.005$. If the mean for all the samples in the sets was 5.103 then the action limits are $5.103 \pm 0.59 \times 0.005 = 5.106$ and the warning limits $5.103 \pm 0.38 \times 0.005 = 5.105$.

Table 5.3 Constants for mean control charts

Sample size	$A'_{0.025}$	$A'_{0.001}$
2	1.229	1.937
3	0.668	1.054
4	0.476	0.750
5	0.377	0.584
6	0.316	0.498
7	0.374	0.432
8	0.244	0.384
9	0.220	0.347
10	0.202	0.317
11	0.186	0.294
12	0.174	0.274

5.7.2 Range control chart for variables

The mean control chart is concerned with control of the mean value of the inspection results obtained for a sample. However, within the sample there may be a wide scatter of the results. A separate control chart, the *range control chart*, is used to control the spread of the values within a sample. The range of values, i.e. the difference between the minimum and maximum values obtained, in the sample is taken and plotted on the range control chart. Figure 5.10 shows such a

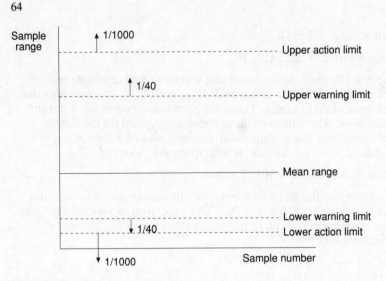

Figure 5.10 Range control chart

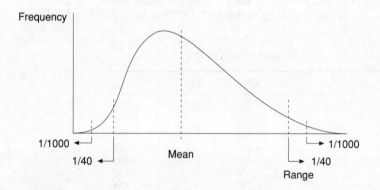

Figure 5.11 Range distribution

chart. As with the mean control chart there are action and warning limits. However, these limits are not symmetrical about the mean range value that is obtained from a number of samples under conditions when it is known that the process is operating satisfactorily. Figure 5.11 shows the form of the distribution of range that might be expected with a purely random variation. As with the mean control chart, tables are available to enable the position of the warning and action limits to be determined.

Upper action limit = $D'_{0.001}\bar{R}$

Upper warning limit = $D'_{0.025}\bar{R}$

Lower warning limit $= D'_{0.975}\bar{R}$

Lower action limit $= D'_{0.999}\bar{R}$

The values of the constants used to multiply the average range depend on the sample size. For example, for a sample size of 5 the constants are $D'_{0.001} = 2.34$, $D'_{0.025} = 1.81$, $D'_{0.975} = 0.37$, and $D'_{0.999} = 0.16$. Table 5.4 gives values of these constants for other sample sizes.

Table 5.4 Constants for range control charts

Sample size	$D'_{0.999}$	$D'_{0.001}$	$D'_{0.975}$	$D'_{0.025}$
2	0.00	4.12	0.04	2.81
3	0.04	2.98	0.18	2.17
4	0.10	2.57	0.29	1.93
5	0.16	2.34	0.37	1.81
6	0.21	2.21	0.42	1.72
7	0.26	2.11	0.46	1.66
8	0.29	2.04	0.50	1.62
9	0.32	1.99	0.52	1.58
10	0.35	1.93	0.54	1.56
11	0.38	1.91	0.56	1.53
12	0.40	1.87	0.58	1.51

Problems

Revision questions

1 What is meant by the term *quality*?
2 What is meant by a company stating they are BS 5750 certified?
3 For a company designing and manufacturing items, what types of information are likely to be included in its quality plan if it is operating to BS 5750?
4 Explain what is meant by *product design quality* and *product manufacturing quality*.
5 List and explain the cost elements involved in quality control.
6 Explain what is meant by *acceptable quality level*.
7 What is meant by the terms *producer's risk* and *consumer's risk*?
8 How does a double sampling plan differ from a single sampling plan?
9 Explain what is meant by *control by attributes* and *control by variables*.
10 Use the binomial expression to determine, for a batch containing a proportion of 0.2 defective items, the chances of a sample of 10 containing 0, 1, 2, 3 defective items.
11 What action, if any, should be taken in the following situations:

(a) The mean value of a sample falls above the upper action limit on a mean control chart for a process.

(b) The mean value of a sample falls between the upper warning limit and upper action limit on a mean control chart for a process.

(c) The mean value of a sample falls between the upper and lower warning limits on a mean control chart for a process.

12 Use Table 5.3 to determine the mean control chart limits for a process which gives, under normal conditions, a mean range value of 10.00. The sample size is 5.

13 Use Table 5.4 to determine the range control chart limits for a process which gives, under normal conditions, a mean range of 10.00. The sample size is 5.

14 Table 5.5 shows the results of inspections of samples of 6 items of a component produced by a machine. Determine the control limits that would apply to the mean and range control charts.

Table 5.5 Problem 14

Sample number	Mean (mm)	Range (mm)
1	100.5	4.2
2	101.0	4.0
3	100.0	4.5
4	100.2	4.0
5	100.8	4.3
6	100.1	3.9
7	100.9	4.1
8	100.1	4.2
9	100.9	3.4
10	100.7	3.7

Case problems

15 The sales department of company ABC has reported to the management team that it is getting frequent requests from customers regarding whether the company is a certified BS 5750 organisation. They feel that they may be losing orders through their lack of knowledge about what this means and the fact that they plainly are not certified. You are thus requested to prepare a paper for the management team which outlines what is meant by this certification and the implications for the organisation of being certified or remaining uncertified. In preparing the paper you visit company DEF which is certified and discuss with your counterpart in that organisation the problems encountered in preparing a similar paper for management. You are told that the lesson that

had been learnt was that the managers would virtually all moan about the cost of implementing such a quality plan and feel that it was throwing money away and there would be no benefit to the organisation or customer. After all they might well have to put up their prices. Address this issue in your paper.

16 The college have set up a company involving the full-time students with the aid of giving them experience of what it might be like working in a company (see Problem 8, Chapter 1). One of the items it is proposed to make is a spanner.

(a) Propose a plan for inspection and hence quality control of incoming materials, the product during manufacture and on completion. Justify your plan. Assume that the spanners are to be made in batches of 50.

(b) It is suggested that statistical quality control methods should be used. Explain how you would set up such a form of control for (i) a stage during the processing, (ii) for the final product.

17 Currently, company XYZ has a problem in that it pursues a policy of rigorous inspection of products after manufacture and 20 per cent of the final manufactured products have to be scrapped or reworked. The large number of final product inspectors and the costs of scrapping and reworking are making the products uncompetitive. You, as a consultant, are brought in to the company to advise it. Write a report detailing your advice.

6 Work systems

6.1 Ergonomics

The term *work system* is used to indicate not only a machine but also the human involved in operating it, being the interaction of human operators and machines in order to do work. The efficiency and effectiveness of the work system in carrying out some operation is affected to the extent to which the operators and machines are matched to each other. For example, an operator working with a lathe may have problems in reaching with ease all the controls. It has been suggested that the controls of the traditional lathe are so situated that, to match with the machine, the ideal operator must be about 1.4 m tall, 0.6 m across the shoulders and have a 2.4 m arm span. The typical male operator is more likely to be about 1.65 m tall, 0.45 m across the shoulders and have a 1.3 m arm span. A mismatch between operator and machine can lead to such problems as fatigue, reduction in operator efficiency, difficulties in obtaining fine control, and consequently a poor standard of work.

There is a need for a machine design to be considered in relationship to the human who is to operate it. Similarly there is a need to consider the human operators when designing a production line. There are constraints on how far a human can reach, how close to each other operators can be placed, the environmental conditions under which they can operate efficiently, etc. For example, the environmental conditions should be such that there is an adequate level of illumination for the operator to see dials on instruments, tool positions, etc., and the temperature should not be too hot or too cold. The human is an integral part of the work system and has to be taken into account in its design.

The term *ergonomics* is given to this study of man–machine and man–environment systems. The aim of ergonomics is to produce well-integrated man–machine and man–environment combinations. A collection of articles which could provide useful background reading is given in *Applied Ergonomics Handbook*, Butterworth, 1974.

6.2 Work station analysis

In considering the design of a work station a logical approach is to consider the human operator as the central key element with the machine, work space and environment being considered relative to the operator. Thus the human is not designed to fit the machine but the machine to fit the human. The human is not designed to fit the work space but the work space to fit the human. The human is not designed to fit the environmental conditions but the conditions designed to fit the human.

The following are thus criteria involved in such a design:

1 the characteristics of the operator, e.g. physique, intelligence, experience, training, motivation, ability to see and respond to signals from instrument displays, ability to use systems to exercise control over a machine;
2 the interaction between the work space and the operator, e.g. the influence on an operator's posture and reach of chairs, desks, machine size, adjacent machines;
3 the interaction between the environment and the operator, e.g. the influence of light levels, colour, noise, heat, smell; in this category psychological effects can be included, e.g. working in teams, shift conditions, night work, pay and welfare.

The following parts of this section highlight some of the features associated with the above.

6.2.1 Characteristics of operators

The characteristics of operators need to be taken into account in the design of any work system. Thus, for example, consideration of an operator carrying out assembly work is likely to need to take into account the height of the seat for the operator relative to the height of the work surface, the location of components within reach of the operator, the location of any visual displays so that they can be easily seen and read without ambiguity, etc.

Table 6.1 shows some of the typical dimensions of adults. The reach of seated adults varies, depending on the direction of reach, both in an

Table 6.1 Typical dimensions of adults

| Characteristic | % of population with dimensions in mm less than | | | | | |
| | Men | | | Women | | |
	5%	50%	95%	5%	50%	95%
Height	1600	1730	1815	1500	1600	1715
Sitting height	840	910	955	785	850	900
Seat breadth	310	360	385	335	360	415
Seat height	430	475	520	420	465	510
Elbow-to-elbow width	375	440	500	335	400	465
Shoulder width	400	445	490	355	400	445

upwards or downwards direction and from side to side. For example, at shoulder height the grasp of the right hand held out horizontally to the right of the body might be 730 mm (measured from the centre of the body) and directly forwards 670 mm. When held upwards at an angle to the horizontal of about 40°, the distance to the right of the body becomes about 600 mm and directly forwards 430 mm. The maximum pulling force that can be exerted on a handle depends also on this distance of reach, being a maximum of typically about 500 N when the arm is extended at the maximum distance of reach and dropping to about half that value at about 40 per cent of maximum reach and 20 per cent when the hand is very close to the body.

6.2.2 Design of displays

The purpose of a display is to transmit information from the machine to the operator. The display might be just a red signal lamp which glows when power is supplied to a machine, or it might be a schematic diagram of a chemical plant with instrument dials and signal lamps at various points on the diagram indicating such variables as temperature, rates of flow and whether various parts are on or off. Most displays involved with production processes are visual, though sound in the form of alarm signals is used in some instances.

Visual displays can be considered to fall into three broad categories:

1 *Qualitative displays*, which enable the operator to distinguish between a small number of different conditions, e.g. whether the power is on or off, whether a valve is open or closed. Such displays typically take the form of signal lights and switches where the position of the knob on the switch indicates, for example, whether the motor is in forward mode, reverse or off.

2 *Quantitative displays*, which present the operator with numerical information, e.g. oil pressure, position of a tool. Such displays can be analogue or digital indicators. With an analogue indicator the position of the pointer on a scale is analogous to the value it

represents; with a digital indicator the information is presented directly in the form of a number. Analogue indicators have the advantage of easily and quickly enabling an operator to see at a glance whether the value is of the right order or moving in the right direction. Digital indicators are particularly good if precise readings have to be logged.

3   *Representational displays*, which provide a diagram mimicking the process or machine and on which information can be displayed indicating the functioning of each part, e.g. a section of a railway system indicating the positions of trains and the settings of signals.

For the typical human, the normal line of sight is straight ahead and about 15° below the horizontal with moderate eye and head movements enabling a circle roughly 10–15° around this to be seen. This defines the optimum area in which visual displays should be located if the operator is not to move in order to extract information from a display.

To enhance the readability of analogue displays the following are some of the criteria generally used (see BS 3693):

1   The scale numbers, scale markings and pointer should contrast in colour with the dial face.
2   Scale numbers should increase in a clockwise direction since this is what operators expect to see.
3   Scales should be numbered in a simple numerical progression, e.g. 0, 1, 2, 3, 4, 5, or perhaps 0, 5, 10, 15, 20, 25, and not in an awkward progression such as 0, 4, 8, 12, 16 or 0, 2.5, 5, 7.5.
4   There should be no more than nine consecutive unnumbered subdivisions.
5   The separation between scale markings should be the same all round the dial; logarithmic or other non-linear scales should be avoided unless absolutely essential.
6   The numbers should be large enough to be read without ambiguity. A simple rule is that the minimum height of a number should be the reading distance divided by 200.
7   The pointer should be visible over most of its length from tip to pivot, with the tip reaching to within 1.6 to 0.4 mm of the scale markings but not overlapping them.

Where there are a number of displays they should be grouped according to purpose and differentiated by colour or by their position. With analogue displays the direction of travel of the pointers should be standardised and the key or normal positions of each display also standardised. Thus if, when conditions were normal, all the displays had their pointers at 12 o'clock then it is relatively simple to see if one is giving an abnormal reading.

6.2.3 Design of controls

The controls are the means by which an operator applies inputs to a machine. The location and form of control used depend on the such factors as the force to be transmitted, the accuracy, speed and range of control required. Table 6.2 shows commonly used controls and their characteristics.

Table 6.2 Controls and their basic characteristics

Type of control	Type of task			
	Force	Speed	Accuracy	Range
Small crank	Very poor	Good	Poor	Good
Large crank	Good	Poor	Very poor	Good
Handwheel	Poor	Poor	Good	Fair
Horizontal lever	Poor	Good	Poor	Poor
Vertical lever, to and from body	Poor when short, good when long	Good	Fair	Poor
Knob	Very poor	Very poor	Fair	Fair
Push button	Very poor	Good	Very poor	Very poor
Rotary selector switch	Very poor	Good	Good	Very poor
Joystick selector switch	Poor	Good	Good	Very poor
Foot pedal	Good	Good	Good	Very poor

Controls need to be located so that they can easily be handled by the operator. When there are a number of controls, the fine adjustment controls should be located as near as possible to the operator, with the coarser ones further away.

6.2.4 Design of workplaces

The design of the workplace means a consideration of the tasks required of the worker: these should be so arranged that injuries and strains do not result from a bad working posture, controls and items should be within easy reach, and displays should be clearly visible. Key factors involved in designing a workplace can be summarised by what are often termed *principles of motion economy*, as

1 Unless it can be avoided, workers should sit rather than stand.
2 The working area should be at the correct height for the worker, a height of about 970 mm can permit both sitting and standing work.
3 Chairs should match the working area height and be adjustable, both the seat height and back rest, to suit the individual worker.
4 Where a high degree of muscular control is required, e.g. with fine assembly work, arm rests should be provided.
5 The working position should only require natural movements of

the body, no undue twisting or reaching over long distances being required.

6 Keep movements symmetrical.
7 The layout should minimise hand, feet and body movements.
8 Mechanical devices should be used to hold a workpiece, rather than the hands being used as clamps.
9 Tools and materials should have fixed locations which permit a constant smooth movement pattern.
10 Power-assisted tools and work-handling equipment should be used wherever possible.

For workers involved in assembly on a production line, the organisation of the work system has a considerable effect on the efficiency of the operation, the workers' morale and strain suffered. Figure 6.1(a) shows the tradition form of work system with all the

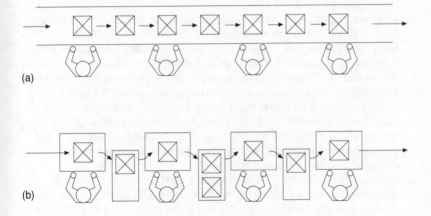

(a)

(b)

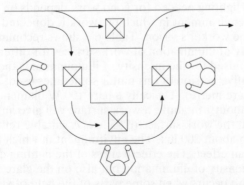

(c)

Figure 6.1 Production line, (a) traditional form, (b) with buffers, (c) with a shunt

workers having to work at exactly the same speed and any faults or interruptions resulting in the entire line coming to a halt. Figure 6.1(b) shows buffers installed between individual workers or groups, such buffers enabling faults or interruptions to the line to have no immediate effect on the line. Figure 6.1(c) shows how work groups can be decoupled from the line by the use of shunts. Different speeds of working of groups can thus be accommodated.

6.2.5 Design of the environment

Thermal comfort is determined by four factors:

1 *Air temperature* The optimum air temperature is about 18°C, though workers who are very active and involved in heavy work may prefer temperatures of the order of 13–16°C while workers engaged in sedentary work, e.g. office workers, may prefer higher temperatures of about 19–22°C.
2 *Radiant temperature* This is the temperature of objects radiating heat with the radiation impinging on the workers. Radiant temperatures should be similar to the air temperatures listed above with workers shielded from high radiant temperatures.
3 *Air humidity* Humidity is a measure of the percentage of moisture required to saturate air at the existing temperature. Very low humidity results in what might be termed a dry atmosphere and can, if temperatures are high, result in discomfort through the drying of the nose and throat. Very high humidity results in what can be termed stuffiness and become particularly evident in crowded and ill-ventilated rooms.
4 *Rate of air movement* With air and radiation temperatures at optimum values, an air circulation of about 150 mm/s is desirable. At this rate the air movement is just perceptible. Air movements above about 500 mm/s are considered very draughty and below about 100 mm/s as airless.

The level of lighting needed for good work depends on the nature of the work, the environment in which the work is done and the sharpness of the worker's vision. Table 6.3 shows recommended values for the intensity of illumination of work surfaces for different types of work. The unit used for the intensity of illumination is the lux (note that an alternative version of this unit is sometimes used, 1 lux = 1 lumen per square metre). Typically a bare 100 W filament electric light bulb situated about 1 m above a work surface will give an intensity of illumination on the work surface of 95 lux. A suitable reflector can increase this to about 200 lux. The environment in which the work is done also has an effect. The effectiveness of the lighting depends not only on the intensity of illumination but also on the glare and contrast produced. Glare occurs when some parts of the field of view are excessively bright in relation to the general level of brightness, e.g. as a consequence of unwanted reflections from polished surfaces. Thus there may be, for example, difficulties in reading the scale on a polished metal surface due to glare from it. Glare can often be reduced by changing the positions of light sources, lowering the brightness of the sources or replacing polished surfaces by matt ones. The directions at which light is incident on an object can affect the contrast between surface details, enabling objects to be distinguished from their background, surface texture to be revealed and markings on surfaces to be more easily seen.

Table 6.3 Recommended levels of illumination

Type of work	Example	Intensity of illumination (lux)
Very fine detail	Assembly of instruments	2000
Fine work	Soldering connections	900
Medium work	Sheet metal work	400
Rough work	Metal stores	200

Noise can not only affect the performance of workers but can also harm their hearing. It is not only intense sounds which can cause deafness, continual exposure over long periods of time to relatively low noise levels can also cause deafness. The unit used for sound intensity is the decibel (dB). The threshold of hearing is 0 dB, a whisper at just over a metre is 20 dB, normal conversation at about a metre is 65 dB, a commercial office is about 70 dB, metal-cutting machines at close range are about 90 dB, a jet taking off at about 200 m is about 120 dB, and a hydraulic press at about 1 metre is 135 dB. For ease of conversion, without shouting, a noise level of more than about 60 dB is undesirable. For work on the shop floor the level of noise that is generally tolerated is about 90 dB. Noise may often be reduced by reducing it at its source, e.g. the mounting of vibrating machinery on isolating mounts to stop the transmission of sound away from the machine. Where this is not possible, operators may be shielded from noise by the use of insulating walls or by the wearing of ear muffs.

6.3 Method study

The term *method study* is used to describe the development of efficient work methods and is one aspect of what is termed *work study*, work measurement being another (see section 6.4). The steps involved in carrying out method study are:

1 *Select* the task to be studied. The most appropriate are those that might produce significant savings as a result of the investigation,

e.g. bottlenecks in the production process.

2   *Record* the existing method of working. This requires observation of the selected task being carried out and a recording of all aspects of it.

3   *Examine* critically the existing method. This involves a consideration of such issues as the purpose of the task, the place and whether it could be done somewhere else, the sequence and whether there are other alternatives, who is doing the task and whether someone else could do it, the means by which the task is done and whether it could be done in some other way.

4   *Develop* an improved method.

5   *Install* the new method, i.e. retrain the workers, provide the new equipment, etc.

6   *Maintain* the new method, i.e. ensure that the task continues to be done in the new way. Follow-up is also necessary in case of unforeseen problems.

In recording the task or tasks a number of charts tend to be used. There are process charts to record the sequence of processes involved in a task, movement charts to record the paths through the work place followed by items involved in a task, multiple-activity charts to show the working–waiting pattern of a group of workers and machines, and two-handed charts to record in detail the movement of each hand in an operation.

Five standard symbols tend to be used in the recording of the sequence of events involved in a process, as shown in Figure 6.2. The symbols can then be combined to give a *process chart* showing the sequence of events. Outline flow charts are used to show the sequence of operations and inspections, thus involving just two of the symbols, whereas flow process charts show all five symbols. Figure 6.3 shows an example of a flow process chart.

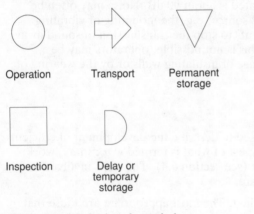

| Operation | Transport | Permanent storage |

| Inspection | Delay or temporary storage |

Figure 6.2   Method study symbols

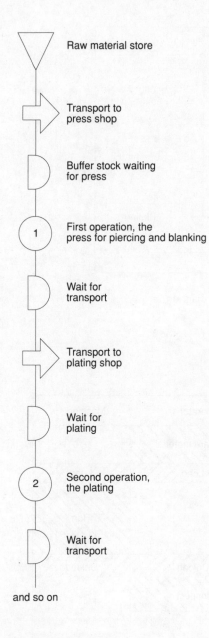

Raw material store

Transport to
press shop

Buffer stock waiting
for press

First operation, the
press for piercing and blanking

Wait for
transport

Transport to
plating shop

Wait for
plating

Second operation,
the plating

Wait for
transport

and so on

Figure 6.3 Flow process chart for a component

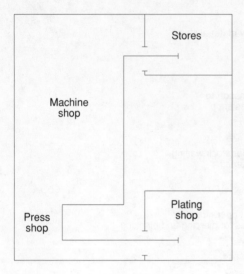

Figure 6.4 A string diagram

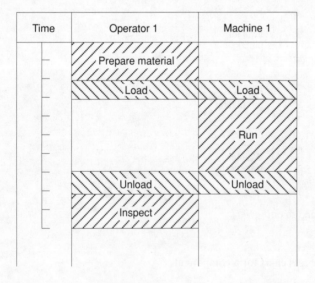

Figure 6.5 A multiple-activity chart

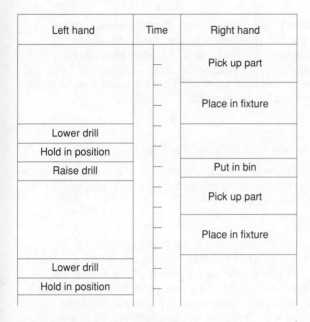

Left hand	Time	Right hand
		Pick up part
		Place in fixture
Lower drill		
Hold in position		
Raise drill		Put in bin
		Pick up part
		Place in fixture
Lower drill		
Hold in position		

Figure 6.6   A two-handed chart

Movement charts are used to show the path followed by items. Such charts show the path on a scale layout of the working area. The term *string diagram* is often used since these diagrams are often constructed using a piece of fine string laid out along the path on a scale layout. The length of the string then gives a measure of the distances moved. Figure 6.4 shows a simple example.

Multiple-activity charts are used to record the time relationships of workers and machines and hence the working–waiting pattern. Figure 6.5 shows an example of such a chart.

Two-handed charts are used to record in detail the movement of each hand of a worker carrying out a task. This can be in the form of just the sequence of operations carried out by each hand, as is shown in Figure 6.6. The movements of each hand might also be recorded on a SIMO chart, SImultaneous MOvement chart. Such a chart shows simultaneously the activity of each hand as a function of time. These charts are generally constructed from a frame-by-frame analysis of a ciné film or video tape of the tasks being carried out.

For a more detailed account the reader is referred to specialist texts, e.g. Whitmore, D.A., *Work Measurement*, Heinemann, 1980.

6.4   Work measurement

The term *work measurement* is used to describe the application of techniques designed to establish the time for a qualified worker to carry out a specified task at a defined level of performance. Such information can be used to plan and allocate plant and labour workloads, to set standards for machine and labour productivity, as the basis for incentive schemes, for costing the labour content of jobs, and to compare different methods of working. There are three main types of methods used for work measurement:

1 Time study
2 Estimating
3 Predetermined motion time systems (PMTS)

The following is a brief account of these methods. For a more detailed account the reader is referred to specialist texts, e.g. Whitmore, D.A., *Work Measurement*, Heinemann, 1980.

6.4.1 Time study

With *time study* the worker carrying out the task concerned is observed. The task is considered as being broken down into a number of small elements, each being a distinct segment of the job. These elements are then timed, generally using a stopwatch. Each element is also rated, the rating being the estimate of the general tempo of the work, taking into account such factors as the effectiveness of the worker and effort expended. The observed rating can then be compared with the standard rating, this being the rate at which an average qualified and motivated worker would work for that element.

There are two basic forms of rating scale, the *Bedaux scale* or 60/80 scale and scales based on 75/100, e.g. the British Standard scale. The Bedaux scale was originally defined so that steady work had a value of 60 and the brisk rate obtained when a worker is working at incentive rate, 80. Bedaux argues that at the steady work rate a worker did 60 minutes of work in an hour and when working at the incentive rate did 80 minutes of work in an hour. The standard rating is now given a value of 80 on this scale. The British Standard scale gives the steady work rate a value of 75 and the brisk incentive rate a value of 100. The brisk rate on both scales is taken as the standard rate. Table 6.4 shows a comparison of the scales. There are problems with inconsistency in applying ratings, since it is very subjective.

Table 6.4 Rating scales

Pace of the worker	75/100 scale	60/80 Bedaux scale
Slow	50	40
Steady	75	60
Brisk	100	80
Fast	125	100
Very fast	150	120

Timing and rating measurements are repeated a number of times in order to obtain reasonable representative data. The basic time for an element is then derived.

$$\text{Basic time} = \text{Observed time} \times \frac{\text{Observed rating}}{\text{Standard rating}}$$

The sum of all the basic times for each element of a task, plus allowances for relaxation and delays for such things as machine adjustments, etc., then gives the standard time for the task. The relaxation allowance is to recognise the fact that a worker cannot sustain a high level of performance without a break in the routine to overcome the effects of boredom and concentration and also the need for periodic resting to recover from physical exhaustion. For example, light bench work by a seated worker may have a relaxation allowance of between 0 and 6 per cent of the observed working time, whereas a worker engaged in very heavy work may have an allowance of 30 to 50 per cent.

6.4.2 Estimating

Estimating is a method of assessing the time required to carry out a task which is based on the knowledge and experience of other similar types of task. No detailed breakdown of the task is made or timings carried out but an estimate made of the time on the basis of: task Y is very similar to task X and so will have a similar time.

The term *analytical estimating* is used when an estimate of the time is obtained partly from knowledge and practical experience of the elements concerned and partly from synthetic data. The term *synthetic* is used because the task is broken down into its constituent elements, or synthesised. Many tasks may be considered to be made up of elements common to other tasks and for which times are known. Thus an estimate may be made of the time for a task on the basis of the times for the common elements, i.e. the synthetic times, without the need to carry out time measurements on the task itself.

The term *comparative estimating* is used when an estimate of the time is obtained by comparing the task with a range of similar tasks, so-called benchmarks, for which times have been measured. The task can then be located within the range of benchmark tasks and an estimate made for its time.

6.4.3 Predetermined motion time systems

Predetermined motion time systems (PMTS) is the technique of work measurement whereby the time for a task is obtained by breaking it down into its basic human motions and using tables of times for each of these motions in order to obtain a time for the task as a whole.

A number of systems have been developed for carrying out such breakdowns of human motions. The most widely used is probably *method–time measurement* (MTM). The MTM-1 system identifies basic motion categories of reach, move, apply pressure, grasp, position, release and disengage. For each of these, tables give times under various conditions of distance, difficulty or load. MTM-1 is capable of giving highly accurate results but is tedious and time-consuming to use. Later versions of the system, e.g. MTM-2 and MTM-3, have a reduced number of categories of motion and are quicker to apply.

6.5 Job analysis

The term *job analysis* is used to describe the analysis of a job. The term *job* is here used to describe the total of what a worker is considered to have to do. Thus a job may be a lathe operator. The term *job description* is used for the statement of the general purpose of a job with an outline of the duties and responsibilities involved. Thus, for example, the lathe operator might have a job description which includes the following:

Title: Lathe operator
Department: Production department
Function: To operate and maintain a lathe in the production of work
    to the specified quality.
Hours of work: 8.30 a.m. to 5.30 p.m. Mondays to Fridays (lunch
    12.30–1.30), plus overtime as required.
Responsible to: Machine shop supervisor
Responsible for/authority over: None
Duties/responsibilities:
1 Comply with company rules, regulations and working practices at
    all times.
2 Comply with instructions received from the machine shop
    supervisor.
3 Maintain tools in good condition.
4 Obtain necessary equipment.
5 Operate the lathe in the production of workpieces, etc.

In order, for example, to determine the training requirements for a job then a *job specification* might be used. This shows the duties involved in a job broken down into tasks, a task being a separate, identifiable activity, with the knowledge and skills required for each task identified. Thus, for example, the duty of maintaining tools in good condition might be broken down into the tasks of: identify the need for resharpening tools, sharpen tools on a grindstone, etc. The tasks of resharpening tools would require the knowledge of types of tools and correct angles of tools with the skills required involving the ability to identify the need for resharpening of different types of tools. On the basis of such a specification the knowledge and skills of an operator can be compared with those required and any gaps identified as training requirements.

For further reading on job analysis the reader is referred to Boydell, T.H., *A Guide to Job Analysis*, BACIE (British Association for Commercial and Industrial Education) 1973, and on training need analysis Boydell, T.H., *The Identification of Training Needs*, BACIE, 1971.

Problems

Revision questions

1 Explain what is meant by the term *ergonomics*.
2 Suggest types of display which would be appropriate for the following situations:
    (a) The operator needs to see at a glance that the power to a machine is on.
    (b) The operator needs to be able to check periodically the value of the oil pressure.
    (c) The operator needs to be able to check whether the motor is off or in forward or reverse motion.
    (d) The operator needs to be able to monitor the performance of a process by taking periodic readings of rates of flow and temperature and keeping a log of the values.
3 Suggest forms of control that could be used in the following situations:
    (a) The operator needs to be able to change the control condition at speed and with accuracy.
    (b) The operator needs to be able to set the position of a tool relative to the tool bed with accuracy but no particular speed.
    (c) The operator needs to be able to quickly exert control in an on–off mode.
4 Consider the variety of types of control used in a car and explain the reasons for each.
5 What are the benefits that might occur from the introduction of buffer zones or shunts in a production line?
6 Explain what is meant by the terms *method study* and *work measurement* and the purposes of each.

Case problems

7 Take a task with which you are familiar, perhaps drilling a hole using a drilling machine, and break it down into (a) suitable time study elements, (b) basic human movements.
8 List the basic human movements involved in picking up a pencil from the table.
9 The workers on an assembly production line have presented, through their shop-floor representative, a list of complaints. Consider them and suggest ways each can be alleviated.
    (a) The different assembly tasks that have to be done mean that

some people can work at a leisurely pace while others have great difficulty in keeping up with the line.

(b) The assembly operation at station C on the line requires a large amount of twisting round on the part of the worker in order to pick up components from racks located at right angles to the work station. This has resulted in back problems.

(c) Part B has to be lifted from the floor and, while not particularly heavy, it seems very heavy by the end of the day and back strain is occurring, slowing down the line.

(d) The worker at station D on the line is having problems in consistently carrying out the fine assembly work because of fatigue developing in his arms.

10 Consider the following scenario. You have been brought in to take a look at the production line in a small company carrying out assembly work and are asked to present a paper proposing modifications which would (a) improve productivity, (b) improve quality and (c) reduce absenteeism. A quick glance at the production line reveals the following situation.

All the workers sit in the work area on standard wooden seats without arm rests, seat adjustments or back rest adjustments. Each of the assembly workers carries out the same assembly operations. Each worker has a series of trays on his or her work area, each tray containing different components, but the arrangement of the trays is entirely up to the worker concerned and they assume an almost random pattern. The work area allocated to each worker is comparatively narrow and since there are quite a lot of trays some can only be reached by stretching. The workpieces have to be held with one hand while components are inserted with the other. When the worker has completed the assembly the workpiece is put onto a conveyor belt which moves behind the line of workers. At the end of the line the workpieces are inspected. This is done by connecting the assembly to a power supply and checking the values given at a range of points when a probe is pressed against them. The inspectors have a single test instrument and probe and satisfactory workpieces give different values at each of the test points. Sometimes the inspectors mistakenly pass a piece when they should have rejected it. This occurs because, though the value indicated by their instrument was a valid one, it was for the wrong test point. When a workpiece is rejected the inspectors have no way of knowing which worker assembled it.

7 Demand forecasting

7.1 Uses of forecasting

Demand forecasting is a vital element in the planning and control of operations. The outcomes of such forecasting will affect the types of product developed and marketed, the production facilities to be provided, the volume of output and inventory levels. Short-term forecasts are particularly useful for production management in order to indicate the expected demand for products and the consequent requirements for materials. Predicting materials requirements is an essential ingredient of production control, since a lack of materials will result in a production hold-up while excessive stocks of materials will be an unnecessary cost. Intermediate-term forecasts provide information on which personnel, equipment and materials requirements can be based for, say, the next year. Long-term forecasts are used to plan the general future of the company, including such items as product mix, exploitation of new products, capacity changes and plant location.

Forecasting techniques can be considered to fall into three categories: those based on opinion; those based on the analysis of historical data; and those based on the analysis of correlation with one or more variables that can be linked to product demand. The analysis of historical data is a technique that is widely used for short-range forecasts, with forecasts based on correlation with linked variables generally being used for short- and intermediate-term forecasting and on opinion for intermediate and long-term forecasting.

The following outlines these techniques. Further reading can be found in books on operational research, e.g. Makower, M.S. and Williamson, E., *Operational Research*, Teach Yourself Books, Hodder & Stoughton, 1975, and more specialist books such as Box, G.E.P. and Jenkins, G.M., *Time Series Analysis Forecasting and Control*, Holden-Day, 1970.

7.2 Forecasts based on opinion

Opinion may be taken from a wide variety of sources, e.g. sales representatives, distributors, customers, the general public. Sales representatives can supply their opinions of such matters as the strength of the competition, customers' attitudes, and sales prospects in their territories. Distributors, because they will probably be selling a range of products, are more likely to present a balanced view than, perhaps, sales representatives. Customer opinion can be gathered by such devices as questionnaires packed with the product while the opinion of the general public can be gathered by market survey.

7.3 Forecasts based on historical data

There are a number of techniques used for making forecasts based on historical data. These include:

1 Drawing the trend line
2 Simple and weighted moving averages
3 Exponential moving averages

7.3.1 Drawing the trend line

Drawing the trend line involves drawing the data on a graph, e.g. annual sales of a product against year or perhaps the number of machine breakdowns against the week, and then from the scatter of points determining the trend line which best fits the data. This line can then be projected forward to give a forecast. At the simplest this trend line can be established by drawing the line by eye. When the trend appears to be a straight line then the best estimate of the line can be made by the use of the *least squares method*.

Suppose we draw some straight lines through the scatter points. For any one point we will have some error between the measured value y and the value predicted y_p by the line (Figure 7.1). Thus the error is $(y_p - y)$ for the value x. The best line is the one for which the sum of the squares of the errors for all the measured points is a minimum, i.e.

$$\Sigma(y_p - y)^2 = \text{a minimum}$$

The process of finding the best line is thus effectively the drawing of

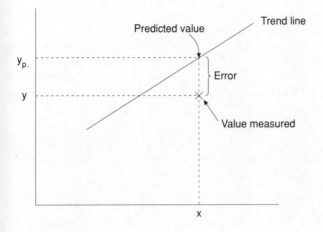

Figure 7.1 Error due to prediction

lines and determining the sums of the squares of the errors for each line until we end up with the line giving the minimum sum of the squares. The term *regression line* is used for the line found by using this condition and the method is called *least squares regression* (note that the word regression has no particular significance now, the original reason for the term being no longer relevant).

In the above we have assumed that the x values are without error and only the y values of the measurement are in error. This gives us what is termed the *regression line for predicting y from x*. We could have assumed that the y values were without error and only the x values were in error. We would then have ended up with the *regression line for predicting x from y* (Figure 7.2).

The general equation of a straight line is

$$y = mx + c$$

where m is the gradient of the straight line and c the intercept of that line on the y axis when x is 0. We thus need to find the values of m and c which result in the minimum value of $\Sigma(y_p - y)^2$, where y_p is the y value of a data point and y the value it would have on the straight line. This is the minimum value of

$$\Sigma(y_p - mx - c)^2$$

and can be obtained by differentiation. From this, for a series of n measurement points $(x_1, y_1), (x_2, y_2), \ldots, (x_n, y_n)$, the gradient m of the best straight line is given by

$$m = \frac{n\Sigma(xy) - \Sigma x \Sigma y}{n\Sigma(x)^2 - (\Sigma x)^2}$$

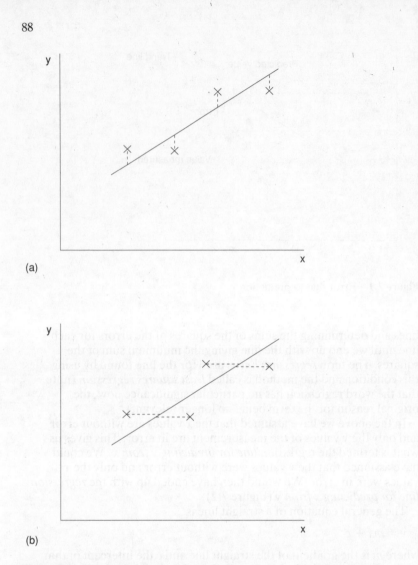

(a)

(b)

Figure 7.2 Regression lines, (a) predicting y from x, (b) predicting x from y

where $\Sigma(xy)$ is the sum of the products of the x and y values for each data point, Σx is the sum of the x values of the data points, Σy is the sum of the y values of the data points, $\Sigma(x)^2$ is the sum of the squares of all the x values and $(\Sigma x)^2$ is the square of the sum of the x values. The intercept c with the y axis, for the best straight line, is given by

$$c = \frac{\Sigma y(\Sigma x^2) - \Sigma x \Sigma(xy)}{n\Sigma(x^2) - (\Sigma x)^2}$$

or

$$c = \frac{\Sigma y - m\Sigma x}{n}$$

The above analysis leads to the identification of the best straight line that can be drawn through data points scattered over a graph. It does not however give any clue as to whether the straight line relationship is a likely one for the set of data. How certain can we be that the relationship is given by the straight line? Is there, in fact, a linear relationship? It might be, for instance, that the data points all fall on some other graphical line, e.g. an exponential curve, and finding the best straight line is not the best way of establishing a relationship for making forecasts. A measure of how well we can be certain of a straight line relationship is the *correlation coefficient r*, where

$$r = \frac{(1/n)\Sigma[(x - \bar{x})(y - \bar{y})]}{\sigma_x \sigma_y}$$

$\bar{x}$ is the mean of the x values and $\bar{y}$ the mean of the y values, σ_x is the standard deviation of the x values and σ_y that of the y values (see section 5.7 for a discussion of the mean and standard deviation). The value of r lies between $+1$ and -1. A value of $+1$ denotes perfect correlation between y and x with an increase in y resulting in an increase in x. Perfect correlation means a straight line graph (Figure 7.3(a)). A value of -1 denotes perfect correlation between y and x with an increase in y resulting in a decrease in x. There is again a straight line relationship between the two quantities (Figure 7.3(b)). When r is 0, there is no correlation between the two quantities concerned. The points on the graph are completely randomly scattered and y does not depend on x in any way. The closer r is to $+1$ or -1 the more the data points cluster about a straight line and we can accept that there is a straight line relationship.

To illustrate the above, consider the determination of the best straight line for predicting y from x for the following data points (in a real situation many more data points would be used):

$$x = 1, y = 2; x = 2, y = 4; x = 3, y = 5$$

x could be batch size, in perhaps hundreds, and y the direct labour costs, in thousands of pounds, and the intention being to determine whether there is a straight line relationship between batch size and labour costs so that forecasts can be made of labour costs for future batches. Alternatively x could be year and y thousands of products sold and the intention being to determine whether there is a straight line relationship between products sold and year so that forecasts can be made for future years.

Table 7.1 shows the steps in the calculation. Thus, with $n = 3$ then least squares regression gives the best straight line as

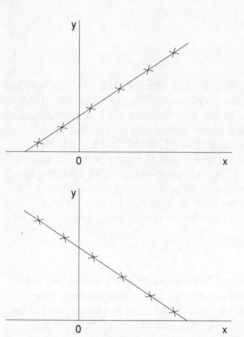

Figure 7.3 Perfect correlation, (a) $r = +1$, (b) $r = -1$

Table 7.1

Month	y	xy	x^2
1	2	2	1
2	4	8	4
3	5	15	9
$\Sigma x = 6$	$\Sigma y = 11$	$\Sigma xy = 25$	$\Sigma x^2 = 14$

Table 7.2

x	y	$x - \bar{x}$	$(x - \bar{x})^2$	$y - \bar{y}$	$(y - \bar{y})^2$	$(x - \bar{x})(y - \bar{y})$
1	2	−1.0	1.0	−1.7	2.89	+1.7
2	4	0.0	0.0	+0.3	0.09	0.0
3	5	+1.0	1.0	+1.3	1.69	+1.3
$\Sigma x = 6$	$\Sigma y = 11$		$\Sigma(x - \bar{x})^2$ $= 2.0$		$\Sigma(y - \bar{y})^2$ $= 4.67$	$\Sigma(x - \bar{x})(y - \bar{y})$ $= +3.0$

$\bar{x} = 6/3 = 2$ $\bar{y} = 11/3 = 3.7$

$$m = \frac{n\Sigma(xy) - \Sigma x \Sigma y}{n\Sigma(x^2) - (\Sigma x)^2}$$

$$= \frac{3 \times 25 - 6 \times 11}{2 \times 14 - 36} = 1.5$$

$$c = \frac{\Sigma y(\Sigma x^2) - \Sigma x \Sigma(xy)}{n\Sigma(x^2) - (\Sigma x)^2}$$

$$= \frac{11 \times 14 - 6 \times 25}{3 \times 14 - 36} = 0.67$$

Thus the best straight line has the equation

$$y = 1.5x + 0.67$$

If we wanted to forecast the value of y when x is 4 then

$$y = 1.5 \times 4 + 0.67 = 6.67$$

How reliable can we consider this estimate? To answer this question we need to determine the correlation coefficient. Table 7.2 shows steps in the calculation.

$$\sigma_x = \sqrt{\frac{\Sigma(x - \bar{x})^2}{n - 1}} = \sqrt{\frac{2.0}{2}} = 1.10$$

$$\sigma_y = \sqrt{\frac{\Sigma(y - \bar{y})^2}{n - 1}} = \sqrt{\frac{4.67}{2}} = 1.53$$

Thus

$$r = \frac{(1/n)\Sigma[(x - \bar{x})(y - \bar{y})]}{\sigma_x \sigma_y}$$

$$= \frac{(1/2) \times 3.0}{1.0 \times 1.53} = 0.98$$

There is thus a high degree of correlation and there is a good chance that the data can be represented by a straight line. Thus the forecast for y when x is 4 is reasonable.

7.3.2 Simple and weighted moving averages

A simple way of smoothing out the effects of random variations in demand is to take a *moving average* value. The average of a set of n data is just the sum of that data divided by n, i.e.

Simple average $\bar{x} = \dfrac{\Sigma x}{n}$

The term *moving average* is used when each time the average is taken it is for the latest n set of data. The set moves forward each time by dropping the earliest piece of data and incorporating the latest piece. For example, sales may be averaged over a period of three months. Thus, at the end of March the sales figures would be averaged over the three months of January, February and March. This average then becomes the forecast for April. At the end of April the sales figures would be averaged over February, March and April, becoming the forecast for May. The January figure has been dropped and the April figure added. At the end of May the sales figure would be averaged over March, April and May, the February figure now being dropped and the May figure added. Thus the forecast F_t for the time t is just the average of the previous n data points

$$F_t = \frac{x_{t-1} + x_{t-2} + \ldots + x_{t-n}}{n}$$

where x_{t-1} is the data value at time $t - 1$, x_{t-2} at time $t - 2$, etc. to x_{t-n} at time $t - n$, thus completing the first period used in the average.

Table 7.3 shows an example of such a three-month moving average. With January sales of 19.5 thousand, February of 20.1 thousand and March of 24.1 thousand then the average for these three months is 21.2 thousand, which is the forecast for the month of April.

Taking a moving average smoothes out random fluctuations and enables a trend to be more clearly seen. Greater smoothing is obtained by averaging over a longer period. Thus a five-month moving average will smooth out random fluctuations better than a three-month moving average.

Moving averages give equal weight to all the data points included in the average. We can, however, weight the data, perhaps by giving

Table 7.3   Three-month moving average

Month	Sales in thousands	Three-month moving average in thousands
January	19.5	
February	20.1	
March	24.1	
April	21.1	21.2
May	20.9	21.8
June	22.0	22.0
July	22.5	21.3
August	26.2	21.8
September	23.1	23.6
October		23.9

Note: The three-month moving average for a set of three months has been entered in the month following the period, i.e. as the forecast for the month following the three. In some situations the average is entered in the mid month of the three or in the last month of the three.

more weight to the latest data and least to the oldest data. Thus, for a three-month moving average we might use the weighting factors 1, 2 and 3. The oldest month is multiplied by 1, the middle month by 2 and the latest month by 3. The weighted moving average is thus the sum of the weighted data for the three months divided by the total weighting, i.e. in this instance 6. For example, with this weighting for sales of 19.5 thousand in January, 20.1 thousand in February and 24.1 thousand in March,

$$\text{Weighted average} = \frac{1 \times 19.5 + 2 \times 20.1 + 3 \times 24.1}{6} = 22.0$$

Table 7.4 shows such a weighting applied to the data used in Table 7.3.

Table 7.4 Three-month weighted moving average

Month	Sales in thousands	Three-month weighted moving average in thousands
January	19.5	
February	20.1	
March	24.1	
April	21.1	22.0
May	20.9	21.9
June	22.0	21.5
July	22.5	21.5
August	26.2	22.1
September	23.1	24.3
October		24.0

Note: The three-month weighted moving average for a set of three months has been entered in the month following the period, i.e. as the forecast for the month following the three. In some situations the average is entered in the mid month of the three or in the last month of the three.

7.3.3 Exponential smoothing

Problems with simple moving averages or weighted moving averages are that there is an arbitrariness about the number of values used in calculating the average. Should we have, for instance, three-month moving averages or five-month moving averages? The calculation of the moving average also involves, each time, a new calculation involving the number of data items being used for the average. The method of *exponentially weighted moving averages*, or *exponential smoothing* as it is often referred to, overcomes these problems. This method uses all the past data points, not just three or five as with three-month or five-month moving averages, and weights all the points with the latest being given most weight. It also enables running calculation to be carried out with just the most recent data point and the forecast for the previous time point.

The weighting factors used with exponential moving averages are, for successive terms,

$$\alpha, \alpha(1 - \alpha), \alpha(1 - \alpha)(1 - \alpha), \alpha(1 - \alpha)(1 - \alpha)(1 - \alpha), \ldots$$

where α is a constant, called the *smoothing constant*, between 0 and 1. With a smoothing constant value of, say, 0.20 then the weighting factors for successive data points are

$$0.20, 0.16, 0.13, 0.10, 0.08, 0.07, 0.05, \ldots$$

The series of weighting factors, an exponential series, has a sum of 1 when summed to infinity.

The forecast F_t for a time t is thus given by

$$F_t = \alpha x_{t-1} + \alpha(1 - \alpha)x_{t-2} + \alpha(1 - \alpha)^2 x_{t-3} + \ldots$$

where x_{t-1} is the data value at time $t - 1$, x_{t-2} at time $t - 2$, etc. This can be written as

$$F_t = \alpha x_{t-1} + (1 - \alpha)[\alpha x_{t-2} + \alpha(1 - \alpha)x_{t-3} + \ldots]$$

But the term in the square brackets is just the forecast F_{t-1} that was obtained for the time $t - 1$ (you can check this by just decreasing all the values of t by 1 in the expression for F_t). Hence we can write

$$F_t = \alpha x_{t-1} + (1 - \alpha)F_{t-1}$$

Thus, remembering that the sum of all the weighting factors is 1, the forecast for a time t is just the weighted average of the most recent data value and the forecast for the previous time point.

The above equation is sometimes written as

$$F_t = \alpha x_{t-1} + F_{t-1} - \alpha F_{t-1}$$
$$= F_{t-1} + \alpha(x_{t-1} - F_{t-1})$$

i.e. the forecast for a time t is the forecast for the time $t - 1$ plus the difference between the actual value and the forecast value at time $t - 1$ multiplied by the smoothing constant.

To illustrate the above, consider the data used in Tables 7.3 and 7.4 with a smoothing constant of 0.4. We will assume that the previous year led to an estimate for January of 19.5 thousand. Then for February we will have a forecast of

February forecast $= 19.5 + 0.4(19.5 - 19.5) = 19.5$

For March we will have a forecast of

March forecast $= 19.5 + 0.4(20.1 - 19.5) = 19.7$

For April we will have a forecast of

April forecast $= 19.7 + 0.4(24.1 - 19.7) = 21.5$

Table 7.5 Exponential moving average

Month	Sales in thousands	Forecasts
January	19.5	(19.5)
February	20.1	19.5
March	24.1	19.7
April	21.1	21.5
May	20.9	21.3
June	22.0	21.1
July	22.5	21.5
August	26.2	21.9
September	23.1	23.6
October		23.4

The results of such calculations are shown in Table 7.5.

It is customary to use fairly small values of the smoothing constant in order to reduce the effects of random fluctuations in demand. A consequence of this is that, though the forecast by this method can follow gradual changes in demand, when there is a sudden change the forecast will lag behind the actual change. To overcome this an *adaptive smoothing system* can be used. The forecast error is monitored and when there are large errors, due to a sudden abrupt change in demand, the value of the smoothing constant is increased so that the system adapts to the new situation. When the demand stabilises then the value of the smoothing constant is reduced so that random fluctuations are filtered out.

7.4 Forecasts based on linked variables

Forecasts can be made on the basis of a mathematical equation which gives the relationship between some quantity which is linked to the variable being studied. Such models can be termed *cause-and-effect* models since data gathered on the cause enables a forecast to be made of the likely effect that will occur. For example, the number of a particular product sold per month might be linked to the selling price of the product by the straight line equation (see section 7.3.1 for a discussion of how such an equation can be arrived at by least squares regression)

$$y = mx + c$$

with y being the number sold and x the selling price. This is referred to as *simple regression*. However, it might be felt that the number sold per month was linked not only to the selling price but also to the amount of money spent on advertising the product. We thus can have what is termed *multiple regression*. The relationship might then take the form

$$y = m_1 x_1 + m_2 x_2 + c$$

where x_1 is the selling price and x_2 the amount of money spent on advertising.

The technique of making forecasts based on linked variables involves establishing the mathematical model, i.e. equation, which links the variable being forecast with other variables.

7.5 Choice of forecasting method

Table 7.6 outlines the basic characteristics of the various methods of making forecasts discussed in this chapter. The decision as to which method to use in particular circumstances will depend on such factors as the accuracy required, whether it is for short-term, medium-term or long-term forecasts, the time and resources available, whether the data is changing rapidly or virtually flat with only random fluctuations, and the sophistication of the managers who are expected to use the results.

Table 7.6 Forecasting methods

Method	Accuracy			Response to change	Cost	Examples of uses
	Short-term	Medium-term	Long-term			
Market survey	Very good	Good	Fair	Fair to good	High	Sales of products
Trend lines	Very good	Fair to good	Very poor	Poor	Low to medium	Inventories, scheduling
Moving averages	Poor to good	Poor	Very poor	Poor	Low	Inventories, scheduling
Exponential smoothing	Fair to very good	Poor to good	Very poor	Poor	Low	Inventories, scheduling
Casual forecasting using regression	Very good	Good	Very poor	Good	Medium	Where strong causal relationships

Because of the significant costs involved in forecasting, a Pareto analysis (see section 4.3.2) might be used to determine which are the most expensive or most used items and for which forecasting becomes more vital than other items. With low-cost items the cost of overstocking is not as significant as it is with high-cost items.

Problems

Revision questions

1 Explain the need for short-, intermediate- and long-term forecasts of demand.

2   Explain how forecasting can be based on the opinion of sales representatives.

3   Explain the techniques that can be used to prepare forecasts based on historic data.

4   Explain the difference between simple and weighted moving averages for the determination of demand forecasts.

5   The demand for an item from the stores is found over the last six months to be

Month	1	2	3	4	5	6
Demand	325	400	375	425	450	425

Use a three-month moving average to forecast the demand for the item and comment on how well the actual demand compares with that forecast.

6   The sales of a product is found over the last 12 months to be

Month	1	2	3	4	5	6
Sales	25	27	24	26	28	27

Month	7	8	9	10	11	12
Sales	34	29	31	29	27	30

Use (a) three-month, (b) six-month moving averages to forecast the sales for the item. Comment on the differences between the two results.

7   Use exponential smoothing with a smoothing constant of (a) 0.1, (b) 0.3 to forecast the demand for the items for which the monthly use was

Month	1	2	3	4	5	6
Use	500	450	510	1000	1050	1000

Month	7	8	9	10	11	12
Use	1100	1050	1100	1000	1050	1100

The forecast for the first month was 500.

8   Use linear regression to determine the relationship between the sales of an item and the advertising expenditure on the basis of the data given in the following table for the last four months:

Month	1	2	3	4
Advertising expenditure	10	20	30	40
Sales	100	190	320	390

Make an estimate of the likely sales if the advertising expenditure is increased to 50.

9   The following table shows the number of units produced each month in relation to the number of shifts worked. If 140 units are required next month, how many shifts should be planned?

Month	1	2	3	4	5	6
Shifts	25	35	15	28	10	20
Units	175	255	100	200	70	150

Case problems

10 The manager of the materials store in company ABC is having difficulties maintaining materials stocks at the right level. Sometimes he runs out of materials, sometimes he is overstocked. He admits that the decisions as to what to order and in what quantities is left to the store supervisor who adopts a policy of ordering when he thinks stocks are getting low and guesses as to what quantities to order.

(a) Present the arguments for a forecasting policy.

(b) Discuss the use that might be made of a Pareto analysis to determine which forecasting method should be used for which material.

(c) Material X is a high-cost item used for a product with a demand which can fluctuate quite widely, material Y is a low-cost item used with a number of products and for which the demand is quite stable, material Z is a medium-cost item for which the demand changes, but not usually at a rapid rate. Advocate forecasting methods for each of the materials.

11 Company FGH is a small company that has been making, for some time, a small range of tool kits for sale through DIY stores. The premises occupied by the company are small and run-down and are scheduled for demolition in a plan for area improvement. The management are thus considering moving to a new industrial estate and the question they face is whether they should go for similar sized premises or for a larger unit to cover a possible expansion. There are several views within the management concerning this and the direction the company should be going in the future. Table 7.7 shows the demand pattern, over the last two years, for the range of tool kits currently produced by the company. The factory currently utilises about 80 per cent of its available space. The income to the company from the sales of the tool kits is tool kit A £70, tool kit B £30, tool kit C £12.

(a) Forecast sales for the immediate future for each of the tool kits.

(b) The sales manager feels the company should drop tool kit A and expand production on the other kits. Discuss this in relation to the contribution made to the company by the various tool kits.

(c) The production manager feels that larger premises would be essential. At present he produces the tool kits in batches and he feels that three parallel production lines would be better. Discuss this in relation to the sales figures and the forecasts for future sales.

Table 7.7 Problem 11

Month	Sales per month		
	Kit A	Kit B	Kit C
1	120	400	900
2	125	410	890
3	130	490	920
4	120	500	920
5	120	520	950
6	125	510	940
7	120	560	930
8	125	600	970
9	130	650	960
10	130	660	970
11	135	670	1000
12	140	650	990
13	145	700	1000
14	140	750	1050
15	140	760	1100
16	140	750	1050
17	135	750	1000
18	140	760	1050
19	140	760	1100
20	145	750	1100
21	150	760	1050
22	150	780	1000
23	155	790	1100
24	160	800	1050

(d) The chief executive feels that the company should add to its range of tool kits and produce a super deluxe kit which would sell for about £150. He certainly would like one. The sales manager feels that a market survey would be necessary. Discuss a possible format for such a survey, who would be asked questions and the types of questions that might be asked.

(e) Give a considered opinion as to whether the company should seek larger premises.

8 Capacity management

8.1 Capacity and utilisation

The term *capacity* is used to describe the resources available for production processes. Such resources include both plant and humans. Thus, for example, the capacity of a process, perhaps a machining cell, is the maximum amount which can be processed in a specified time. Thus a machine and operator, which are available for productive work of h hours per day and d days per year and on which each product unit requires a time of p hours, have a capacity of hd/p units of product per year. If there are n such machines in a cell then the capacity is nhd/p units per year. Capacity can thus be defined as

$$\text{Capacity} = \frac{\text{Time available in a specified time}}{\text{Time to make one unit}}$$

If there is more capacity than is required, then the capacity is not fully utilised and we can define the *utilisation* as

$$\text{Utilisation} = \frac{\text{Capacity available}}{\text{Capacity used}}$$

or as the equivalent definition

$$\text{Utilisation} = \frac{\text{Time used for production}}{\text{Time available for production}}$$

8.1.1 Capacity with a process layout

With a process form of layout (see section 3.3.1) all the plant and labour associated with a particular type of process are grouped together. Thus there may be a group of lathes with associated operators, a group of drills with associated operators, etc. Products are routed between the different groups of machines according to the sequence of processes they require. Working with batches, it is possible for machine group A to complete all its work on batch 1 before the batch is passed to machine group B. While machine group B is working on batch 1, machine group A can be working on batch 2. Thus, production control involves the timing of the routeing between the various groups of machines so that each group can be utilised to its full capacity.

8.1.2 Capacity with a production line

Consider a production line, i.e. a product layout (see section 3.3.1), involving three successive processes, as illustrated in Figure 8.1. Process A has a capacity of 100 units per working day, process B a capacity of 120 units per working day, and process C a capacity of 90 units per working day. The limiting constraint on the production is obviously process C and thus the capacity of the flow layout is 90 units per working day. If there was only a throughput of 70 units in a day then the utilisation is 70/90 = 0.78 or 78 per cent.

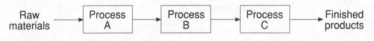

Figure 8.1 Production line

Suppose we have a flow layout involving three processes with the first process consisting of three machines, each having a capacity of 20 units per working day, the second process consisting of two machines, each having a capacity of 25 units per day, and the final process a single machine with a capacity of 70 units per day. The capacity at each of the process stages is thus: first stage, 60 units per working day; second stage, 50 units per working day; third stage, 70 units per working day. The limiting constraint is thus set in this example by the second stage. The overall capacity of the flow line is thus 50 units per working day. Only when this capacity is operated at each stage will work flow in a continuous sequence through the various stages of the production line.

8.2 Capacity planning

The term *capacity planning* is used for the planning of the capacity of an organisation to meet the expected demand. The process of capacity planning thus involves the forecasting of future demands, the translation of the forecasts into physical capacity requirements, the consideration of how the requirements can be met and finally the establishment of a plan for implementation.

There are some products which can be considered to have mature, stable markets. The term *mature* implies that the market is not changing and rapid changes in technology or fashion are not occurring. The term *stable* implies that there is an almost constant demand for the product. The common electric light bulb might be regarded as an example of such a product. With such products an organisation can make forecasts of future demands by extrapolating trends or by using mathematical techniques to smooth out the random fluctuations and arrive at a forecast (see Chapter 7).

With new products, or products in a rapid development phase, or products subject to rapidly changing technology or fashion, or where competition is fierce, then the forecasting of future capacity requirements is more difficult. For example, the forecasting of the demand for a particular model of computer over, say, the next 10 years is extremely difficult since the technology is changing very rapidly and there is fierce competition. Thus with such uncertainty with regard to

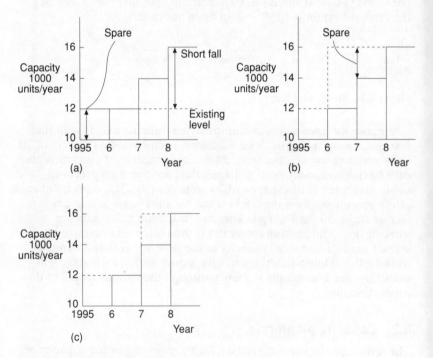

Figure 8.2 Capacity planning

future demand, capacity planning requires an assessment to be made of the risks involved. How much money will the company lose if it plans for a forecast future demand and the actual demand is less? How much money would the company lose if the actual demand is greater than the forecast?

Consider an organisation planning for capacity requirements, for a product in a reasonably mature, stable market. Suppose, for example, the forecasts are

Year	1995	1996	1997	1998
Capacity in units per year	10 000	12 000	14 000	16 000

If the initial capacity is, say, 12 000 units then in 1995 there will be some spare capacity, but in later years the capacity will be insufficient (Figure 8.2(a)). Consideration thus has to be given to how to cope with this problem. Extra capacity might mean enlarging existing facilities with an extra capacity of 4000 units per year coming on-line in 1996 (Figure 8.1(b)). This would lead to an excess of capacity in 1997. Alternatively, it may be that some demand could be met by subcontracting some work, using overtime or multiple shifts, etc., and the enlargement of the facilities could wait until 1997 (Figure 8.1(c)). Such an arrangement would lead to less spare capacity. Spare capacity costs money. A shortfall of capacity can also cost money in terms of lost sales. Thus the aim is to have just the right amount of capacity to give 100 per cent utilisation.

8.2.1 Capacity adjustment

The ideal situation is a 100 per cent utilisation of capacity. However, fluctuations in capacity requirements are likely to occur and measures have to be taken to cope with such fluctuations. There are two basic strategies that can be used: chase demand and level capacity.

With a *chase demand* strategy the capacity is adjusted to respond to demand changes. This adjustment might involve

1 using overtime, changes in shift working, or lay-offs
2 hiring and firing employees
3 using part-time labour
4 subcontracting work.

With a *level capacity* strategy the capacity is maintained constant and variations in demand are absorbed by

1 allowing stocks to build up or run down
2 allowing orders to build up, or even turning down orders.

Often a mixture of the two strategies may be used.

Seasonal fluctuations in demand might be met by chase demand and/ or level capacity strategies. Additionally, differential pricing arrangements might be used in order to reduce peak demand and increase off-peak demand, advertising might be directed towards increasing off-peak demand, and complementary products might be developed which have countercyclic seasonal trends. For example, it is reputed that Walls, which sold sausages, developed an ice cream trade so that the summertime sales of ice cream complemented the wintertime sale of sausages.

8.2.2 Capacity planning costs

When considering capacity planning the following costs need to be considered:

1 *Hiring and firing costs* The cost of hiring a new employee has to include the recruiting and training costs needed to bring the new employee up to full productive skill. Firing costs include such items as severance pay.
2 *Overtime costs* The overtime costs are the normal wages plus a premium and thus products produced during overtime cost the company more money than those during normal time.
3 *Extra shift costs* Extra shifts involve not only extra worker costs but also costs for all the support facilities required – extra maintenance costs of the plant, extra management costs, etc.
4 *Part-time labour costs* While part-time labour might be obtained at a cheaper hourly rate than full-time labour, they may well not have the experience of the full-time labour and so be less productive. Full-time labour will still, however, be needed for supervision.
5 *Inventory costs* Costs are incurred as a consequence of an organisation carrying stocks of products. Such costs include the cost of the capital needed, the costs of storage, the costs of deterioration, etc.
6 *Subcontracting costs* It is often more expensive to subcontract the work than to produce the goods within the company.
7 *Backlog or refusing orders costs* The cost for increasing the delivery time of goods to customers, or refusing orders, might be a loss of customers, particularly in situations where there are competitors.

The capacity planning aim is to determine a plan which minimises costs. Mathematical models have been devised to aid in this achievement.

Problems

Revision questions

1 Explain what is meant by the *capacity* of a process.
2 Explain how the capacity of a production line can be computed

from the capacities of each of the processes in the line.

3 A machining cell has n machines, each working for h hours on each of s shifts per day, with their being d working days per year. If the total number of product units produced per year is p, what is the capacity of the cell?

4 List some techniques that might be used to (a) increase, (b) decrease production capacity.

5 Explain how a company might cope with changing capacity requirements which are seasonal.

6 Explain how a company might adjust demand in order to maintain constant capacity.

Case problems

7 Company ABC produces to a seasonal demand with the forecast for the next 12 months as follows:

Month	1	2	3	4	5	6
Demand	200	220	300	400	500	600

Month	7	8	9	10	11	12
Demand	400	300	200	150	100	100

The labour force, with no overtime and with the existing plant, can produce 250 units per month, the cost per unit being £100. With overtime the number of units produced can be increased to 300 per month, the extra units each costing £120. Subcontracting for up to 50 units per month is feasible, the cost of these being £140 per unit. The cost of a lost sale is reckoned to be £20. Propose, and justify, a plan for the company to meet the demand every month without changing its present labour force and plant.

8 Company FGH makes bicycles. The demand for bicycles is seasonal with the main sales being for shops stocking up for Christmas. Over the next 12 months the demand is forecast to be as follows:

Month	Jan.	Feb.	Mar.	Apr.	May	June
Demand	200	200	250	300	350	400

Month	July	Aug.	Sept.	Oct.	Nov.	Dec.
Demand	450	500	600	500	350	250

The management have decided to consider three capacity plans: adjustment of inventory levels to meet peak demands; using overtime to meet peak demands; hiring part-time workers for peak demand times. Evaluate these strategies on the basis of the following data:

(a) The inventory at the beginning of the year is 250 bicycles and the aim is to have the same size inventory at the end of the next year.

(b) The throughput of bicycles is 3 bicyles per month of regular time working per worker employed. Each worker costs £2000, taking into account support services.

(c) On overtime the same production rate can be assumed, with a maximum of 20 per cent overtime in any one month being feasible. Overtime costs are 150 per cent of normal work time.

(d) Part-time workers can each contribute 1 bicycle per month and their labour costs £1000 per month per worker, taking into account support services.

(e) The cost of producing a bicycle is £50 and the cost of carrying stock is £1 per bicycle per month.

9 Project network analysis

9.1 Projects

This chapter is about an aid to the planning of projects, the term *project* being used for any self-contained piece of work. Such pieces of work contain a number of activities. The term *activity* is used to describe a task requiring time and resources for its completion. The planning of a project requires a consideration of the activities that constitute the project, the order in which they must be done, the timing of each activity and the resources needed at each stage.

As an illustration, consider the making of a cup of instant coffee. This project involves a number of activities such as putting water in the kettle, switching on the kettle, getting a cup from the cupboard, getting the instant coffee from a cupboard, getting a spoon from a drawer, using the spoon to put coffee in the cup, switching off the kettle when the water boils, pouring water on the coffee, etc. The planning of the project of making a cup of coffee requires a consideration of the order in which the activities are done. Thus there is no point in switching on the kettle until water has been put into it, or of pouring water on the coffee until the water has boiled. Getting the cup and the coffee could be done before or after switching on the kettle; however it must be done before the water is poured on the coffee. Each of the activities will take a certain amount of time. Thus by considering the timing of each, it is possible to determine the time at which the boiling water will be poured on the coffee, and how long it will take to make the cup of coffee. The timing of the resources required for each activity can then be ascertained.

9.1.1 Project network analysis

Project network analysis is a technique that has been evolved to help in the planning of projects. The technique was developed independently and almost simultaneously by two groups in the 1950s. One group, at E.I. du Pont, developed the technique they called *critical path method* (CPM) as an aid to the planning of the maintenance of chemical plants. The other group developed the technique they called *project evaluation and review technique* (PERT) for the United States Navy for the planning of the development activities for the Polaris missile programme. The CPM and PERT techniques are based on essentially the same concepts, the original difference being that CPM was based on fixed times for each activity while PERT was based on probabilistic estimates of activity times. Today the two techniques tend to be combined in one approach, with fixed or probabilistic times being used. The technique is often called *critical path analysis* (CPA).

Project network analysis

1   presents information relevant to the planning of a project in an easily understandable form
2   identifies the order in which activities should be done and their interdependence
3   identifies the time by which each activity must be finished if a delay in the completion of the project is not to occur
4   identifies the maximum delay in each activity that will not result in delay within the entire project
5   shows which activities are most critical to the completion of the project
6   provides an estimate of how long a project will take
7   allows scheduling of resources to meet the requirements of the activities
8   enables monitoring and control of the activities during the project.

The technique is used for such projects as the construction of roads, bridges, ships, buildings, the launch of new products, the manufacture of one-off items, and plans for plant maintenance.

Commercial computer software is available to carry out project network analysis. For example, the software Project 3.0 by Microsoft enables such analysis and develops network charts. Gannt charts can be produced and resource levelling carried out.

9.2 Constructing networks

The rail or underground network is often illustrated on paper, with each station represented by a small circle and lines drawn between the circles to indicate which stations are linked by rail lines. The circles, i.e. the stations, represent the points in the network where the event of getting on or off trains occurs, the lines show the sequence of stations through which the train must pass in order to get from the start station to the final destination. Each line between two stations represents the activity of going between the stations and has a time. Project networks are drawn in a similar way.

In a project network each *activity* is represented by an arrow. The length of an arrow has no particular significance, though its direction does, indicating the direction of progress of the activity. Each activity is represented by one and only one arrow in the network, no single activity can be represented twice and no two activities can be represented by the same arrow (see the later discussion of dummy activities). The network is constructed by drawing all the activities in the order in which they have to be done. The beginning and end points of each activity are described by two events. An *event* represents a point in time and is represented by a small circle. To aid identification the events are numbered, the sequence of numbers, however, having no particular significance. The precedence relationships between activities are thus described by the events, i.e. when each activity starts and when it finishes. Figure 9.1 illustrates the above for an activity linking events 1 and 2.

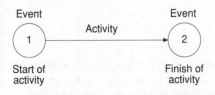

Figure 9.1 An activity occurring between two events

The basic rules that are used in drawing networks are:

1 A network has only one starting and one finishing event.
2 Each activity is represented by only one arrow in the network.
3 Any two events can only be connected by one activity.
4 No two activities can be identified with the same head and tail events.
5 Each event has a unique identifying number.

To ensure the correct precedence relationships in the network diagram each activity has to be considered in relation to the activities that must be completed immediately before it can start, the activities that must follow it, and the activities that must occur concurrently. Figure 9.2 shows two simple examples. Figure 9.2(a) shows three sequential activities A, B and C. Activity A has to be completed before activity B can start. Activity B has to be completed before activity C can start.

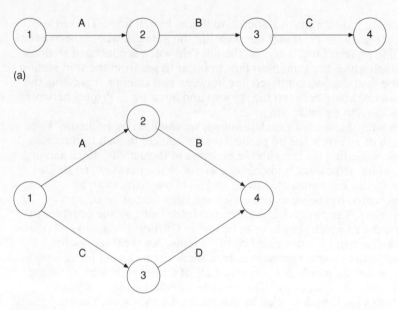

(a)

(b)

Figure 9.2 Examples of networks, (a) sequential activities, (b) parallel activities

Figure 9.2(b) shows parallel activities. Activity A has to be completed before activity B can start. Activity C has to be completed before activity D can start. Activities A and C can start at the same time but the activity which follows on from B and D cannot start until both B and D have been completed.

There are some situations which cause problems in drawing networks and deriving information from them. Any two events must only be connected by one arrow, i.e. there cannot be two activities starting and finishing at the same time. Consider the situation where

activity B depends on activity A
activity C depends on activity A
activity D depends on activities B and C

The network for this would seem to be that shown in Figure 9.3(a), but this would have two events connected by more than one arrow. The way round this problem is to define a *dummy activity*. Figure 9.3(b) shows how Figure 9.3(a) can be drawn with a dummy activity included. The dummy activity, shown by the dotted line, has zero duration and requires no resources. Another situation where a dummy activity is used is when we have

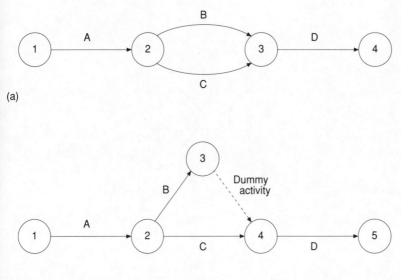

(a)

(b)

Figure 9.3 (a) Incorrect network, (b) correct network using a dummy activity

activity C depends on activity A
activity D depends on activities A and B

Figure 9.4(a) cannot really represent this situation. Figure 9.4(b) shows how it can be represented by the use of a dummy activity.

To illustrate the application of the above principles in the construction of a network, consider the following example which might be the activities involved in, say, the manufacture of a one-off product by a small engineering company.

Activity A depends on no previous activity
Activity B depends on no previous activity
Activity C depends on activity A
Activity D depends on activity A
Activity E depends on activity C
Activity F depends on activity D
Activity G depends on activity B
Activity H depends on activity G
Activity I depends on activities E and F
Activity J depends on activities H and I
Activity K depends on activity J

Figure 9.5 shows the network diagram. Activities A and B have no predecessors and thus can start immediately. They can thus both start from the same start event 1, though it should be recognised that they

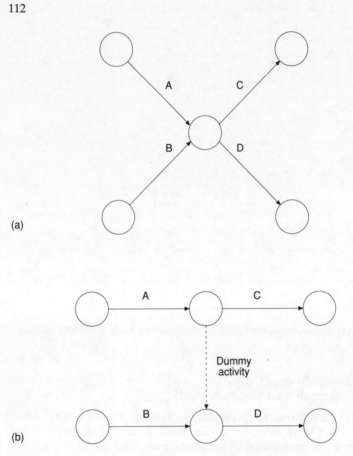

Figure 9.4 (a) Incorrect network, (b) correct network using a dummy activity

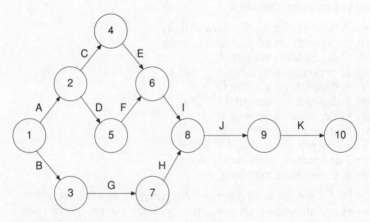

Figure 9.5 Network example

need not start at the same time, only that they must be complete before the activities which depend on them can start. Activities C and D depend on activity A and thus both start at event 2 which is at the head of the arrow representing activity A. Activity E depends only on activity C and thus is sequential with that activity. Activity F depends only on activity D and is thus sequential with that activity. Activity I depends on activities E and F and thus we must have activities E and F terminating at a unique event 6 which can then act as the starting event for activity I. Activity G depends only on activity B having been completed and thus is sequential with that activity. Activity H depends only on activity G having been completed and thus is sequential with that activity. Activity J depends on activities I and H having been completed. Thus activities I and H must end in a unique event 8 and activity J can then start from that event. Activity K depends only on activity J and is thus sequential with it. The unique start point for the network is event 1 and the unique end point is event 10.

9.3 Timing of project activities

The analysis of the times of events in a network is an important feature of planning of a project. Consider the activities specified by Table 9.1. Figure 9.6 shows the resulting network and the following outlines the calculations involved in determining

1 the earliest start time for an activity
2 the earliest finish time for an activity
3 the latest start time for an activity
4 the latest finish time for an activity.

Consider the *earliest start times* and *earliest finish times* for activities. Activity A has a duration of 3 units of time and does not depend on any previous activity. Thus the arrow denoting this activity has an earliest start time of 0 and an earliest completion time of 3. Activity C depends on activity A and has a duration of 4 units of time. Thus, since the earliest completion time for activity A is 3 then the earliest start time for activity C is 3 and the earliest completion time is 7. Since the activity E has a duration of 2 units of time and it depends only on activity C then the earliest start time is 7 and the earliest completion time is 9. Activity B has a duration of 2 units of time and does not depend on any other activity. Thus the arrow denoting this activity has an earliest start time of 0 and an earliest completion time of 2. Activity D has a duration of 3 units of time and depends on activity B. Thus its earliest start time will be 2 and its earliest completion time 5. Activity F depends on activity D and has a duration of 1 unit of time. Thus the earliest start time for the activity is 5 and the earliest completion time 6. Activity G depends on activities E and F. The earliest completion time of activity E is 9 and the earliest completion time of activity F is 6. Activity G cannot start before both activities E and F are complete

114

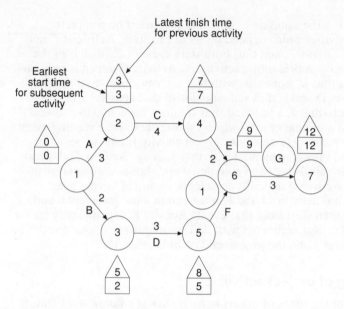

Figure 9.6 Network with earliest start times and latest finish times

and thus cannot start before time 9. Activity G has a duration of 3 units of time and thus the earliest completion time is 12.

The earliest start time for each activity is calculated from the beginning of the network by totalling all the preceding activity durations. When two or more activities lead into one event then the following activity cannot begin until both of the preceding activities are completed and consequently the last of the activities to finish determines the earliest start time for the subsequent activity.

The *latest finish times* for activities are calculated by working backwards from the end event of the project by successively subtracting activity durations from the project finish time. Thus, with Figure 9.6, starting at event 7, the latest finish time at event 6 must be

Table 9.1 Data for timing example

Activity	Depends on	Duration
A		3
B		2
C	A	4
D	B	3
E	C	2
F	D	1
G	E and F	3

Table 9.2 Times for example in Table 9.1

Activity	Duration	Earliest start time	Earliest finish time	Latest start time	Latest finish time
A	3	0	3	0	3
B	2	0	2	3	5
C	4	3	7	3	7
D	3	2	5	5	8
E	2	7	9	7	9
F	1	5	6	8	9
G	3	9	12	9	12

9, i.e. 12 − 3. This must be the latest finish time for both activities E and F. The latest finish time at event 5 must be 8, i.e. 9 − 1. Hence the latest finish time for activity D is 8. The latest finish time at event 4 must be 7 and hence this is the latest finish time for activity C. The latest finish time at event 2 is 3 and hence this is the latest finish time for activity A. When two or more activities stem from one event, then the latest finish time for that event is determined by the earliest of the latest finish times for the previous activities.

The *latest start time* for an activity is calculated by subtracting from the latest finish time the duration time of that activity. Thus, for example, activity F, which has a latest finish time of 9 and a duration of 1, has a latest start time of 9 − 1 = 8. This is in fact the latest finish time of the previous activity.

Figure 9.6 shows the earliest start time for the subsequent activity and the latest finish time for the previous activity at each of the events, these being the times usually entered on network diagrams. The convention is generally adopted of putting the earliest start time for the subsequent activity in a square box and the latest finish time for the previous activity in a triangular box. Table 9.2 summarises the times derived above.

9.3.1 Floats

For some activities the difference between the earliest start time for an activity and the latest finish time for that activity is greater than the required duration of the activity. Thus, for example, for activity D in Figure 9.6 the earliest start time for that activity is 2 units of time while the latest possible finish time for the activity is 8 units. There is thus a possible duration for the activity of 8 − 2 = 6 units. The duration of activity D is 3 units. Thus there is some leeway regarding the duration of activity D. This leeway is referred to as the *total float* and is the difference between the time available for an activity and the time actually used.

Total float = Latest finish time for an activity minus the earliest start time for it minus its duration

For some activities there are no floats. Such activities are critical in that they must be completed on time if there is to be no delay in the overall project and it is to finish on time. Thus a *critical activity* is defined as one having zero total float.

The term *free float* is used to indicate the leeway of time that is possible for an activity when all activities start as early as possible.

Free float = Earliest start time of following event minus the earliest start time of preceding event minus the activity duration

Thus, for activity D the free float is $5 - 2 - 3 = 0$. For activity F it is $9 - 5 - 1 = 3$. The free float must be zero when the total float is zero, but the free float may be zero when the total float is not zero.

9.3.2 Critical path

The *critical path* through a network is the longest duration path and defines a chain of critical activities that connect the start and end events. Any delay in the activities in the critical path will delay the completion of the project. In Figure 9.6 the critical path is the path through events 1, 2, 4, 6 and 7 involving activities A, C, E and G.

To illustrate the above, consider a project for the installation of a new process. Table 9.3 shows the activities involved in the project, their durations and dependences. Figure 9.7 shows the resulting network with the earliest start times and latest finish times indicated. Table 9.4 shows these times and the derived floats. The critical path is through activities A, B, D, F, I and J. All these activities have zero total float. The duration of the critical path is the sum of the durations of these activities, which is 57 days.

Figure 9.8 shows an example of a network involving a dummy activity. Such an activity has a duration of 0. Table 9.5 shows the resulting table of times and floats. The critical path is though activities B, D, the dummy and F and has a duration of 13 units of time.

Table 9.3 Machine installation example

Activity	Description	Duration in days	Depends on
A	Determine machine specification	8	
B	Design machine base and facilities	5	A
C	Order machine	3	A
D	Order materials for base and facilities	2	B
E	Wait for machine to be delivered	12	C
F	Wait for base materials, etc.	8	D
G	Train machine operators	4	A
H	Employ company to install base, etc.	3	B
I	Install base and facilities	20	F, H
J	Install machine	14	E, G, I

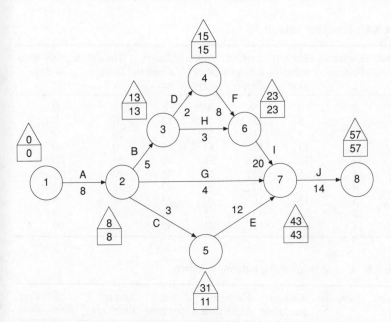

Figure 9.7 Machine installation example

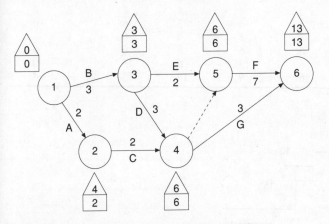

Figure 9.8 Example involving a dummy activity

9.4 Gannt chart

The result of network calculations regarding times is generally the construction of a chart which shows the activities plotted against a time scale. Such a chart is referred to as a *Gannt chart* (Figure 9.9). This figure shows the machine installation example given by Tables 9.3 and 9.4 and illustrated by the network in Figure 9.7. The solid horizontal

Table 9.4 Times for Table 9.3

Activity	Duration in days	Earliest start in days	Earliest finish in days	Latest start in days	Latest finish in days	Total float in days	Free float in days
A	8	0	8	0	8	0	0
B	5	8	13	8	13	0	0
C	3	8	11	28	31	20	0
D	2	13	15	13	15	0	0
E	12	11	23	31	43	20	20
F	8	15	23	15	23	0	0
G	4	8	12	39	43	31	31
H	3	13	16	20	23	7	7
I	20	23	43	23	43	0	0
J	14	43	57	43	57	0	0

Table 9.5 Example involving a dummy activity

Activity	Duration	Earliest start time	Earliest finish time	Latest start time	Latest finish time	Total float	Free float
A	2	0	2	2	4	2	0
B	3	0	3	0	3	0	0
C	2	2	4	4	6	2	2
D	3	3	6	3	6	0	0
E	2	3	5	4	6	1	1
Dummy	0	6	6	6	6	0	0
F	7	6	13	6	13	0	0
G	3	6	9	10	13	4	4

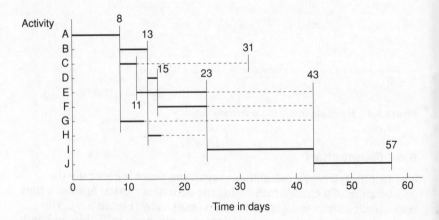

Figure 9.9 Gannt chart

line for an activity indicates the duration of the activity between its earliest start and earliest finish times. Where there is a total float, this is shown by the dotted extension to the solid line. Thus the figure shows that activity A must occur between days 0 and 8, it being a critical activity with no float. Activity C, however, is not critical and has an earliest start of 8 days and earliest finish of 11 days but there is a total float of 20 days and no delay to the overall project will occur provided the activity is completed before 31 days.

A Gannt chart clearly shows the activities which should be occurring at a particular time, those which should have been completed and those which are due to start. It thus enables the progress of the project to be easily checked.

9.4.1 Resource levelling

The Gannt chart enables resource allocations to be planned. Critical activities are ones for which there are no floats and so must occur within fixed times. Non-critical activities do however have some total float and thus the start can be delayed to the extent of the float without affecting the overall finish time for the project.

For example, for the Gannt chart shown in Figure 9.9, up to day 8, A is the only activity. Then activities B, C and G can start. Activity B is critical and so must start at day 8. However, activities C and G can have their starts delayed. Thus if we felt that we could not cope with more than two activities occurring at a given time then, say, activity G could be delayed to a later time. It must however be completed before day 43 if the project is to finish on time. Thus activity G might, for instance, be rescheduled to occur between days 23 and 27. By such considerations it is possible to use the floats to level the resources over the duration of the project in order to avoid peaks and troughs in resource requirements.

The procedure that can be adopted for resource levelling is thus:

1 Schedule all activities for their earliest start times and find the resources needed throughout the project.
2 For those times when too many resources are required, delay non-critical activities to times when less resources are required. If the total float equals the free float then a non-critical activity can be scheduled anywhere between its earliest start and latest finish times. If the free float is less than the total float then the starting time of the non-critical activity can be delayed relative to its earliest start time by no more than the amount of the free float if the scheduling of its immediately succeeding activities are not to be affected.

To further illustrate the above, consider another example. Figure 9.10(a) shows the Gannt chart for a project. Table 9.6 shows the number of workers involved in each of the activities in the project. Figure 9.10(b) shows how the number of workers used in the project will vary through it when all activities are scheduled for their earliest start times. Figure 9.10(c) shows how some levelling can be achieved by moving the non-critical activity F to weeks 3 to 5. Further adjustments of those activities with floats can result in even more levelling.

9.4.2 Costs

The duration of an activity depends on the amount of resources allocated to it. Thus, often the duration of an activity can be reduced if more resources are used. Figure 9.11 shows the type of relationship that is generally assumed. Reducing the duration from its normal value increases the cost with their being a lower limit to the duration, called the *crash duration*, below which the duration cannot be reduced. The costs referred to in the figure are the direct costs only, indirect costs such as those relating to premises, administration and supervision are not included.

Table 9.6 Number of workers required per activity

Activity	Number of workers
A	0
B	4
C	6
D	3
E	8
F	4
G	4
H	6

Suppose we want to reduce the time taken for a project. Only those activities in the critical path affect the overall project duration. In order to obtain a reduction at the least possible cost, the critical activity with the smallest slope of its cost–time graph should be chosen. The amount by which the duration of such an activity can be reduced is determined by its crash limit. The result of reducing the duration of a critical activity is a new schedule and possibly even a new critical path. If further reduction is required then the critical activity in the new schedule with the smallest slope of its cost–time graph can be chosen and its duration reduced. Another new schedule will be produced. This procedure can be repeated until the required duration is obtained.

Figure 9.12 shows the effects on the cost of a project by such a step-by-step reduction of critical activities to their crash limits. The direct costs rise as the project duration is reduced. It seems logical to expect that the greater the duration of a project, the higher will be the indirect costs. The total cost of a project will be the sum of the direct

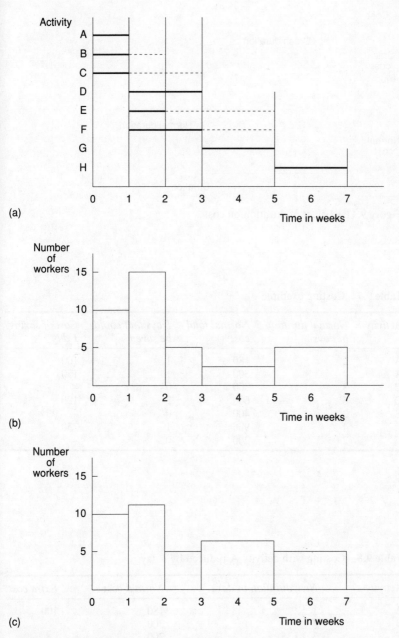

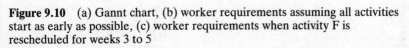

Figure 9.10 (a) Gannt chart, (b) worker requirements assuming all activities start as early as possible, (c) worker requirements when activity F is rescheduled for weeks 3 to 5

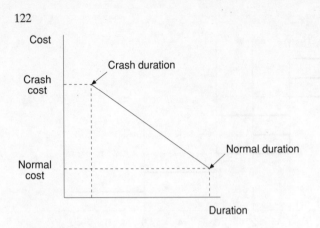

Figure 9.11 Effect of duration on cost

Table 9.7 Costing example

Activity	Normal duration in days	Normal total cost	Days that could be saved	Cost of saving 1 day
A	2	180	1	100
B	4	300	1	150
C	3	300	0	–
D	6	600	2	120
E	2	400	0	–
F	4	900	1	250
G	2	200	0	–

Table 9.8 Costing with activity A reduced by 1 day

Activity	New duration in days	Normal cost	Extra cost
A	1	180	100
B	4	300	
C	3	300	
D	6	600	
E	2	400	
F	4	900	
G	2	200	

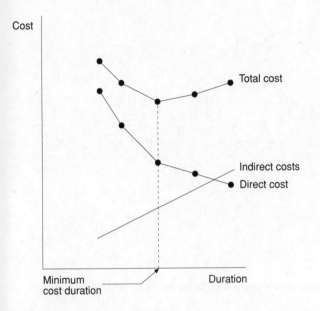

Figure 9.12 Project costs

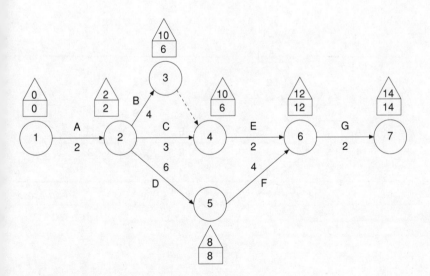

Figure 9.13 Network example, critical path ADFG

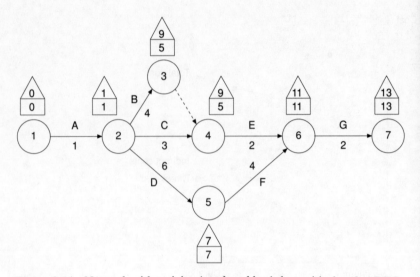

Figure 9.14 Network with activity A reduced by 1 day, critical path ADFG

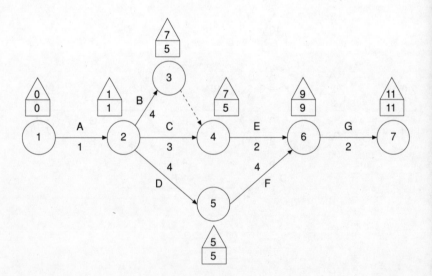

Figure 9.15 Network with activity D reduced by 2 days, critical path ADFG

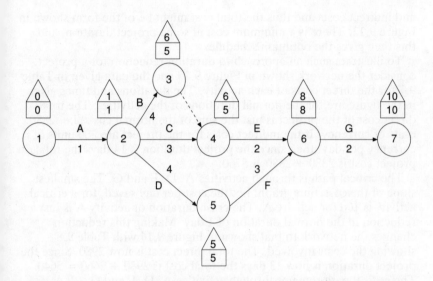

Figure 9.16 Network with activity F reduced by 1 day, critical path ADFG

Table 9.9 Costing with activity D reduced by 2 days

Activity	New duration in days	Normal cost	Extra cost
A	1	180	100
B	4	300	
C	3	300	
D	4	600	240
E	2	400	
F	4	900	
G	2	200	

Table 9.10 Costing with activity F reduced by 1 day

Activity	New duration in days	Normal cost	Extra cost
A	1	180	100
B	4	300	
C	3	300	
D	4	600	240
E	2	400	
F	3	900	250
G	2	200	

and indirect costs and thus the total cost might be of the form shown in Figure 9.12. There is a minimum cost at some project duration, and this then gives the optimum schedule.

To illustrate such an approach to duration reduction for a project, consider the network shown in Figure 9.13 and the data given in Table 9.7 for the direct costs of each activity. The durations and times given in the figure are for the normal durations of the activities. The total direct cost of the project is just the sum of the normal costs, i.e. 2880 units of currency. If the indirect costs for the project are 200 units of currency per day, then since the project duration is 14 days the total project cost is 2880 + 2880 = 5760.

The critical path is through activities A, D, F and G. The smallest slope of the cost–time graph, i.e. the cost per day saved, for a critical activity is 100 for activity A. The crash duration of activity A is just a reduction in the normal duration of 1 day. Making this reduction changes the network to that shown in Figure 9.14 with Table 9.8 showing the costs involved. The total direct cost is now 2980. Since the project duration is now 13 days the total cost is 2980 + 2660 = 5640. The critical path remains through activities A, D, F and G.

The next smallest slope of the cost–time graph for a critical activity is 120 for activity D. The crash duration of activity D is a reduction of 2 days from the normal duration. Making this reduction changes the network to that shown in Figure 9.15 with Table 9.9 showing the costs involved. The total direct cost is now 3220. Since the project duration is now 11 days the total cost is 3220 + 2200 = 5420. The critical path remains through activities A, D, F and G.

The next smallest slope of the cost–time graph for a critical activity is 250 for activity F. Note that although activity B has a smaller slope it is not a critical activity and so a reduction in its duration has no effect on the overall duration of the project. The crash duration of activity F is a reduction of 1 day from the normal duration. Making this reduction changes the network to that shown in Figure 9.16 with Table 9.10 showing the costs involved. The total direct cost is now 3470. Since the project duration is now 10 days the total cost is 3470 + 2000 = 5470. The critical path remains through activities A, D, F and G.

The optimum network is that shown in Figure 9.15 since this gives the lowest total cost for the project.

Problems

Revision questions

1 What information is needed to draw a project network?
2 Explain the meaning of the terms *activities* and *events* in project networks.
3 What are dummy activities? Give an example of when one might be used.

4 Explain how the earliest start and finish times, and the latest start and finish times, for activities can be determined.

5 What is meant by the term *total float* of an activity?

6 What is a critical path?

7 Draw the network which can represent the following relationships:

Activity A depends on no previous activity
Activity B depends on no previous activity
Activity C depends on activity A being completed
Activity D depends on activity B being completed
Activity E depends on activity D being completed
Activity F depends on activities D and C being completed
Activity G depends on activity F being completed.

8 Draw the network which can represent the following relationships (note that a dummy activity is required):

Activity A depends on no previous activity
Activity B depends on activity A being completed
Activity C depends on activity A being completed
Activity D depends on activity A being completed
Activity E depends on activity B being completed
Activity F depends on activities C and D being completed
Activity G depends on activity D being completed
Activity H depends on activities E, F, G being completed.

9 Draw the network which can represent the following relationships (note that a dummy activity is required):

Activity A depends on no previous activity
Activity B depends on activity A being completed
Activity C depends on activity A being completed
Activity D depends on activity B being completed
Activity E depends on activity B being completed
Activity F depends on activities D and E being completed
Activity G depends on activity C being completed
Activity H depends on activities F and G being completed
Activity I depends on activity H being completed.

10 Draw the network, indicating the earliest start time for the subsequent activity and the latest finish time for the previous activity at each event, for the data given in Table 9.11.

11 Explain what a Gannt chart is and how it can be constructed from network data.

12 Construct a Gannt chart for the network specified by Tables 9.1 and 9.2.

13 Construct a Gannt chart for the network specified by the data given in Question 10.

14 Explain how a Gannt chart can be used for resource levelling.

15 Explain the significance of the slope of the cost–duration graph for

Table 9.11 Problem 10

Activity	Duration in days	Depends on
A	5	
B	4	A
C	6	B
D	2	A
E	4	D
F	8	E
G	3	
H	8	G
I	5	H and J
J	9	
K	8	A
L	2	C and K
M	4	I and L
N	5	M and F

Table 9.12 Problem 16

Activity	Depends on	Duration in days	Normal cost	Days that could be saved	Cost for saving 1 day
A		3	360	1	120
B	A	2	240	1	80
C	A	4	660	2	90
D	B and C	3	160	–	
E	D	2	180	1	80
F	A	15	600	2	140
G	E	1	150	–	
H	F and G	3	300	1	180

critical activities in determining the effect of reducing the duration of a project.

16 For the data given in Table 9.12 for a project, (a) draw the network diagram for normal durations of the activities and determine the normal duration of the project, the critical path and the total cost, and (b) determine how the total cost of the project depends on its duration and hence determine the optimum duration which gives minimum cost. The indirect costs amount to 130 units of currency per day.

Case problems

17 The RST company is a small manufacturing company which makes small, cheap, items for other companies to use as promotional 'toys' to give to potential customers. The company designs the items, manufacturers them, markets them to

companies, and usually customises them by embellishing them
with the name of customer companies. The 'toys' generally have a
fairly short life-cycle before new ones have to be designed. As
soon as the sales of a 'toy' begins to decline the company has a
policy of introducing a new one. There is thus a frequent change
of products. The 'toys' are generally fairly simple and involve only
very simple technology. The time between and initial design and
product marketing is generally about 100 days.

The company is concerned with the competition and is looking
to ways by which the time needed to introduce a new 'toy' can be
reduced, and project network analysis has been suggested as a
way of analysing the procedure. On the basis of the following
information for a typical new 'toy', use project network analysis to
examine it and produce a case study which can be used by the
management to see the potential of the method.

The initial design takes 15 days. Following this, production
prototypes are made, requiring 14 days. The prototypes are then
used in a market survey with the company representatives visiting
a number of existing customers. This takes 5 days. Following this
the design team takes 5 days to produce the revised specification.
Concurrently with this the production department can be engaged
in training workers on the basis of the prototype for the new
product, 3 days being required, and the packaging design team
can be designing the packaging, 3 days being required. The
packaging design is sent out to specialist manufacturers for tender,
12 days being required for this. When the best tender is accepted
the order is placed and the packaging made. This takes 20 days.
Prior to starting up full production, the production process is
planned. This planning can start after the prototype has been
produced and takes 12 days. When the final design specification is
ready, 3 days are needed to make adjustments to the production
plan and set the machines. First a small batch of samples is
produced to test the process and overcome teething problems.
This takes 3 days. Then finally production and the packaging of
the product occurs, with 10 days needed to produce a sufficient
quantity for stock. A sales leaflet is prepared following the
redesign after the prototype and is sent out when the products are
in stock. The design of the leaflet takes 2 days and the preparation
of the artwork 3 days. The leaflet is printed in-house, taking 2
days.

18 Take an electric mains plug to pieces and work out the network
that describes the operations involved in assembling such a plug
from its constituent parts.

10 Production planning

10.1 Pre-production planning

Pre-production activities form an important part of production planning and can include

1 capacity planning
2 monitoring of factory loads and adjustment of capacity to meet loading requirements
3 design work
4 process planning
5 determining the requirements for bought-in components and materials
6 determining labour requirements, both numbers and training.

The most long-term element in the pre-production planning phase is capacity planning (see Chapter 8). This involves the planning of the capacity requirements against forecasts of demand. Later, when orders are received, capacity adjustments may need to be made (see section 8.2.1). Other pre-production planning depends, to some extent, on the type of production system concerned.

There can be considered to be four basic types of production systems:

1 Finished goods are stocked and the customer is served from those stocks. The term *subcontractor* is often used. When an order is

received the main pre-production activity is likely to be process planning. The efficiency of the operation will depend on (a) knowledge of the mix of work on hand and where and when there is spare capacity, and (b) the ability to schedule the work so that reliable delivery dates can be given and that all sections of the factory are loaded as fully as possible.

2 Goods are made for stock and the customer is served from stock. When goods are made for stock then the products are ordered from the production department against forecast sales or as a consequence of a stock control policy to maintain certain levels of stock.

3 Goods are made against a customer's order from standard materials already held in stock in the company, production only starting when an order has been received. An example of this is a company which makes an item for which customers can have small changes made in order that the item fits their own particular needs. With the making of goods from standard materials against a customer's order, then, in the sequence of pre-production activities, the order can be received after virtually all the process planning has occurred and can be considered to be just a fine tuning of process plans.

4 Goods are made against a customer's order, with materials having to be obtained when the order is received. For this form of production the pre-production planning has to include such activities as design work, preparation of drawings and specifications, preparation of process plans, possibly tool design and manufacture, purchase of materials and bought-in components, etc.

10.2 Activity scheduling

One of the main activities of production planning is activity scheduling. This, in simple terms, can be considered to be the timing of activities so that customer demand is met on the due date with an efficient flow and co-ordination of activities occurring in the production organisation.

Scheduling in production systems where there is no buffer of stock between the production facility and the customer is likely to be primarily against a target delivery date for the customer, and thus a schedule might be determined by working backwards through the activities from that date. When the production is for stock the scheduling is likely to be primarily determined by the aim of maximising productivity by an efficient loading of production departments and plant in order to ensure that stock levels are maintained within some predetermined bands (see Chapter 13). Thus the issue can become one of which job should be done next. (See Chapter 11 for a discussion of batch scheduling and Chapter 12 for scheduling of flow processing.)

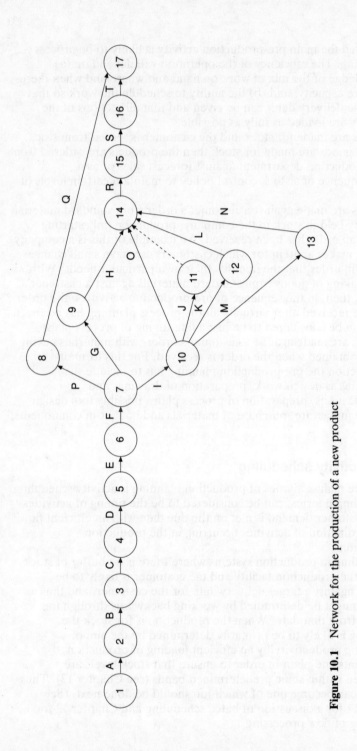

Figure 10.1 Network for the production of a new product

Schedules can be shown in the form of Gannt charts (see section 9.4). Such charts show when each activity is to occur and thus can be used as progressing documents, enabling the progress of products to be compared with that necessary for the schedule to be met.

10.2.1 Manufacture of a new product

To illustrate the above, the following are the activities that can be involved in the introduction of a new product for sale from stock.

A   Market survey to disclose the requirements for the product.
B   Design the product.
C   Produce a prototype of the initial design.
D   Test/market test the prototype.
E   Revise the design if necessary.
F   Produce drawings and specifications.
G   Obtain quotations for bought-in parts.
H   Place orders for bought-in parts and wait for delivery.
I   Plan production methods for in-house made parts.
J   Design and manufacture tooling.
K   Obtain quotations for manufacturing equipment not already available.
L   Place orders for equipment and wait for delivery.
M   Obtain quotations for materials which have to be bought and are not already in store.
N   Place orders for materials and wait for delivery.
O   Train production workers, recruiting extra if necessary.
P   Design promotion materials for new product.
Q   Promote the new product.
R   Carry out trial production to iron out any teething problems.
S   Manufacture the new product.
T   Deliver to product warehouse to await orders.

Some of the above activities cannot start until another activity (or activities) has been completed. Thus, for example, activity C cannot start until activity B has been completed. In some cases, activities can occur concurrently. Figure 10.1 shows one form the project network could take (see Chapter 9 for an explanation of networks).

The above activities might be broken down into a number of sub-activities and networks drawn for them. Thus, for example, in an electrical product activity B, concerning the design of the product, might involve

B1   Designing the power supply
B2   Designing the main electrical circuit
B3   Designing the case.

Activity C, the production of the prototype, might involve the following activities:

C1 Obtaining the materials for the case
C2 Obtaining the electrical components
C3 Making the case
C4 Assembling the circuit boards
C5 Testing the circuit boards
C6 Assembling the prototype
C7 Inspection of the prototype.

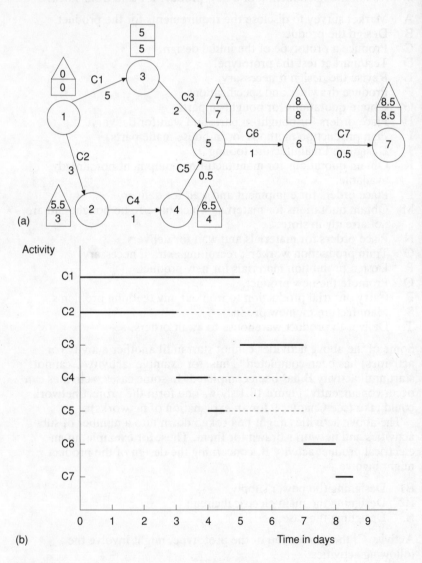

Figure 10.2 (a) The network diagram, (b) the Gannt chart

Table 10.1 Manufacture of the prototype

Activity	Duration in days	Depends on
C1	5	–
C2	3	–
C3	2	C1
C4	1	C2
C5	0.5	C4
C6	1	C3 and C5
C7	0.5	C6

Network diagrams can be used to develop Gannt charts (see section 9.4). Thus, as an illustration, Figure 10.2 shows the network and Gannt chart for the activities involved in the production of the prototype and Table 10.1 represents the relationships and durations of the activities. The total duration of that stage of the project is 8.5 days with the critical path being through the activities C1, C3, C6, and C7. There is thus no slack in the timing for those critical activities but some for activities C2, C4 and C5. The network and Gannt chart also enable expenditure and resource requirements at different times during the project to be ascertained and adjusted (see section 9.4.2). Thus, for example, if resource requirements were stretched during week 4, then activity C5 could be moved to the following week without affecting the overall duration of the project.

Problems

Revision questions

1 Describe the four general systems in which production companies can be classified.
2 Outline the main pre-production activities with which subcontractors would be likely to be involved.
3 Outline the main pre-production activities with which a company making items for stock would be likely to be involved.
4 List the activities likely to be involved in the production of a product, against a customer's order. Draw the project network diagram.
5 Explain how network diagrams and Gannt charts can be used as progressing documents.

Case problem

6 Company ABC makes two types of product, one type is non-standard items against orders and the other is standard items for stock. The following are the activities involved in the company making non-standard items against orders. Construct an

appropriate network diagram. Also produce a modified form of the network to cover the making of standard items for stock and delivery to customers from stock.

A Order received and logged.
B Order passed to production scheduling for scheduling.
C Material requirements determined.
D Process details and plant loading requirements determined.
E Details of material requiring to be purchased sent to the purchasing department.
F Purchasing department obtains quotations from suppliers.
G Materials ordered from suppliers.
H After some period of time the materials are delivered.
I The incoming materials are inspected.
J The materials are then put into store.
K Materials are released from store when requested for manufacturing.
L The materials move to the production department buffer store.
M The materials are drawn from the buffer store for process operation 1 and the process undertaken.
N After operation 1 the partly manufactured product moves into work-in-progress storage.
O Process operation 2 is undertaken.
P After operation 2 the partly manufactured product moves into work-in-progress storage.
Q Process operation 3 is undertaken.
R After operation 3 the finished product moves to inspection where it queues for inspection.
S The product is inspected.
T The inspected product moves to finished goods storage.
U The finished product is logged as inventory.
V The finished product is moved to the dispatch department.
W The product waits in a queue in dispatch.
X The product is packed.
Y The product waits for shipping.
Z The product is shipped to the customer.

11 Batch processing

11.1 Batch processing

Batch processing can be considered to include such systems as the production by batch of items for stock, the processing of batches through a machine or machine shop to another machine or machine shop, the grouping of customers' orders so that the batches of items are taken from stock and shipped, and the grouping of customers' orders for production in batches. Production planning with batch processing requires a consideration of batch sizes, batch sequencing and batch scheduling. In other words, what quantity of items or customers should be processed at one time, in what order should batches of different items or customers be processed, and what should be the timing of the processing of the different batches?

The following is a consideration of these questions. For further consideration the reader is referred to texts on operational research, e.g. Makower, M.S. and Williamson, E., *Operational Research*, Teach Yourself Books, Hodder & Stoughton, 1975.

11.2 Batch sizes

Consider the question of what quantity of items should be processed at one time. Batch quantities which are too small will result in low stock levels and the need for frequent processing of small batches to keep up with demand. This will result in extra costs being incurred as a result of the extra ordering costs, preparation and setting-up costs, etc. Batch quantities which are too large will result in high stock levels and the extra associated costs, such as capital tied up in stock, the costs of stock-keeping, depreciation, etc., these being referred to generally as holding costs. The batch size at the minimum total cost is termed the *economic batch quantity* (EBQ) or the *economic order quantity* (EOQ).

11.2.1 Minimum cost batch size

Consider the situation where items are delivered into stock as a complete batch at the end of a processing period. The stock is then allowed to run down as customers' orders are supplied. The same variations in stock are obtained if we consider components being bought-in and delivered in batches, with the components then being drawn from stock at a gradual rate as they are required in the processing of a product. For simplicity we will assume that the run down of the stock is at a constant rate. The stocks are run down until a certain stock level is reached, then another batch is delivered. This minimum stock level is termed the *buffer stock*. The variation of stock with time is thus as shown in Figure 11.1.

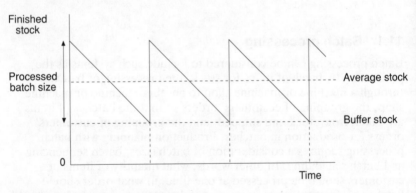

Figure 11.1 Batch size and stock levels

Consider the way in which the number of items in stock decreases with time, before restocking occurs. If the number of items delivered in a batch to stock is Q and the rate at which items are taken from stock is r items/unit time, then the time t taken to use a batch is rt/Q. If C_s is the setting-up costs per batch, then the costs incurred per batch, and in a time t, are $C_s rt/Q$.

The average stock is

$$\text{Average stock} = \frac{1}{2}Q + B$$

where B is the buffer stock level. If C_h is the holding cost per item per unit time, then over a period of time t the holding cost will be

Holding cost $= \left(\frac{1}{2}Q + B \right) C_h t$

The total cost over a time t is thus

$$\text{Total cost } C = \frac{C_s rt}{Q} + \left(\frac{1}{2}Q + B \right) C_h t$$

$$= \left(\frac{C_s r}{Q} + \frac{QC_h}{2} + BC_h \right) t$$

The minimum cost value can be obtained by differentiating the above equation to give

$$\frac{dC}{dQ} = -\frac{C_s r}{Q^2} + \frac{C_h}{2}$$

The minimum occurs when $dC/dQ = 0$, and so the minimum cost batch size, the EBQ, is when

$$\text{EBQ} = \sqrt{\frac{2C_s r}{C_h}}$$

The minimum cost per unit time is with this EBQ batch size, and substituting this value of EBQ into the cost equation gives

$$\text{Min. cost} = \sqrt{(2C_s C_h r)} + BC_h$$

Figure 11.2 shows how the holding cost, the setting up cost and the total cost vary with time.

The processing cycle time, i.e. the time which elapses between successive batch deliveries, is

$$\text{Process cycle time} = \frac{Q}{r}$$

Thus the processing cycle time when the batch size is the economic batch size is EBQ/r.

Consider the situation where a manufacturer needs 10 000 of a particular component per year. Each batch has a machine set-up cost of £200 and the stock-holding cost per component is £4 per year. What will be the size of the batches which will give minimum cost? The rate r at which components are taken from stock is 10 000 per year. Thus, assuming that batches are delivered in their entirety into stock

$$\text{EBQ} = \sqrt{\frac{2C_s r}{C_h}} = \sqrt{\frac{2 \times 200 \times 10\ 000}{4}} = 1000$$

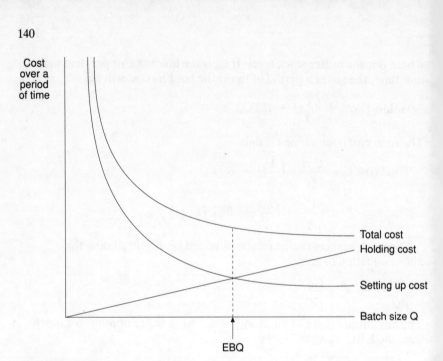

Figure 11.2 Costs and batch size

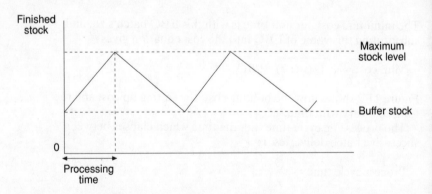

Figure 11.3 Replenishment of stock occurring over a period of time

The manufacturer should thus produce the 10 000 components in batches of 1000.

11.2.2 Minimum cost batch size with gradual replenishment

The above discussion was of a situation when all the items in a batch are delivered into stock at the same time. Figure 11.3 shows the situation which can occur when the items in a batch are delivered into stock continually throughout the processing time. If the rate at which items are delivered from processing to stock is q then the processing time, i.e. the time taken to deliver the batch size of Q, is Q/q. However, while items are being delivered to stock, items are also being withdrawn from stock. Thus, if r is the rate at which items are withdrawn from stock then the maximum stock level is the batch size Q minus the number of items withdrawn during the time taken to produce a batch, plus the buffer stock size B. The number of items withdrawn during the time Q/q is rQ/q. Thus

$$\text{Max. stock} = Q - \frac{rQ}{q} + B = Q\left(1 - \frac{r}{q}\right) + B$$

The average stock is B plus the average of $Q(1 - r/q)$ and is thus

$$\text{Average stock} = \frac{Q}{2}\left(1 - \frac{r}{q}\right) + B$$

The holding cost over a period of time t is thus

$$\text{Holding cost} = \left[\frac{Q}{2}\left(1 - \frac{r}{q}\right) + B\right]C_h t$$

where C_h is the holding cost per item per unit time. The setting-up cost over the time t is, as before, rtC_s/Q when C_s is the setting-up cost per batch. Thus the total cost during a time t is

$$\text{Cost } C = \frac{rtC_s}{Q} + \left[\frac{Q}{2}\left(1 - \frac{r}{q}\right) + B\right]C_h t$$

Except for the factor $(1 - r/q)$ this is the same as the cost equation in 11.2.1 for batches delivered in an entity on completion. The minimum occurs when $dC/dQ = 0$, and so the minimum cost batch size, the EBQ, is

$$\text{EBQ} = \sqrt{\frac{2C_s r}{C_h(1 - r/q)}}$$

The processing time is Q/q and thus, at the economic batch quantity, is EBQ/q.

11.3 Buffer stocks

Buffer stocks are held in order to:

1 Cover differences between actual and forecast demands. This could be the difference between the sales demand and the forecast demand for a product. It could also refer to a processing sequence for a batch of products when the output from machine A is different from that forecast and buffer stocks are needed to enable

machine B in the processing sequence to operate at full load.

2   Cover late deliveries of in-company processed products into store.
3   Cover final inspection, turning back some items as not being of the right quality.
4   Cover deliveries of bought-in materials and components being late or under the required amounts.

11.4   When to order?

There are two basic policies that can be adopted:

1   *periodic review* when new orders for batches are issued at equal intervals of time
2   *continuous review* when new orders are placed when the stock level reaches some re-order level.

With continuous review the re-order level depends on the level of usage of the item concerned. Thus, for example, the re-order level might be set at when the stock level drops to 2 months' average usage, the stock is then topped up by the economic batch quantity. With periodic review the optimum order interval is

$$\text{Optimum order interval} = \frac{\text{EBQ}}{\text{Usage rate}}$$

This issue of when to order is discussed in more detail in Chapter 13.

11.5   Sequencing

Sequencing is concerned with the determination of the order of job processing for machines. For example, suppose we have a number of batches of different products waiting to be machined. In what sequence should the batches be machined? The following are some of the criteria used for determining the sequence.

1   First come, first served. This means that the batch which arrives first at the work centre is processed first.
2   In order of length of processing time. The batch with the shortest processing time is processed first. This means that since the quickest jobs are completed first, other machines which are concerned with later processes on the product will receive work and so have a higher utilisation.
3   In order of due date for completion. The batch with the earliest completion date is processed first.
4   In order of the least slack time. The slack time is the time to the due date minus the processing time. A job with zero slack time would thus only have just enough time to be processed if it is to be completed on time.
5   In order of the runout time, the batch with the lowest runout time

being taken first. The runout time is the current stock level divided by the average demand.

6   In order of the queue at the next operation, the batch with the smallest queue at the next operation being taken first.

To illustrate the above, consider a situation where there are five batches queuing for a particular machine and the sequence is to be decided by runout times. Table 11.1 gives the data for the stock levels and average demand for the products in each of the five batches. The runout time for product A is thus $40/5 = 8$. For product B the runout time is $12/4 = 3$. For product C the runout time is $50/10 = 5$. For product D the runout time is $28/4 = 7$. For product E the runout time is $20/5 = 4$. Thus the sequence is B, E, C, D, A.

Table 11.1 Runout sequencing example

	Product				
	A	B	C	D	E
Average demand/week	5	4	10	4	5
Current stock	40	12	50	28	20

11.6 Scheduling

Consider the situation where a company is manufacturing goods for stock, and suppose demand forecasts indicate that they will need by the end of week 10 a stock of 20 of item A, and by end of week 11 a stock of 10 of item B. The procedure that is followed is that *works orders* are issued to authorise production for each item. A works order for item A would specify a job number, say 1001, the product as being item A, the quantity required, i.e. 20, and when delivery is required, i.e. week 10. The production control department is then responsible for determining a route and schedule for the manufacture of the item. The works order is thus responsible for triggering production planning for an item and thus is the critical document in exercising control over which items start the production sequence leading to manufacture.

Production planning involves considering for each work order the work content. For example, job number 1001 for the production of 20 of item A by the end of week 10 might have the work content of

Department 1, 3 days with 1 operator
Department 2, 2 days with 1 operator
etc.

Job number 1002 for the production of 10 of item B by the end of week 11 might have the work content of

Department 1, 4 days with 1 operator
Department 2, 3 days with 1 operator
etc.

The problem is how to schedule the jobs so that the loading on any one department is kept within its capacity.

Thus, for just the two jobs 1001 and 1002 outlined above, consider department 1. A first attempt at a schedule might be done by ignoring capacity limitations and seeing what develops. Thus we could schedule job 1001 through its sequence of departments to its completion date. If the schedule indicates a total job duration of, say, 3 weeks then the job must start at the latest by week 7 in order to be completed by week 10.

We could now schedule job 1002 through its sequence of departments to its completion date. If the schedule indicates a total job duration of, say, 4 weeks then the job must start at the latest by week 7 in order to be completed by week 11. Thus in week 7 the requirements for department 1 are 3 operator-days for job 1001 and 4 operator-days for job 1002. Suppose for argument that the capacity of department 1 is limited to 5 operator-days in a week. Then clearly both jobs cannot be completed in department 1 in week 7. If we follow the sequencing rule of the order being determined by the due date of delivery, earliest date being first, then job 1001 would be tackled before job 1002. Thus we might then schedule job 1001 to go to department 1 in week 6 and job 1002 in week 7. This would enable the delivery dates to be met.

The above example essentially involved determining a schedule by working backwards from the completion dates, initially ignoring any capacity restrictions. Then when conflicts with existing capacity are found the schedule is adjusted to take account of them. Such an adjustment can be by adjusting the dates by which production starts, or is completed, or by increasing available resources by overtime, subcontracting, etc.

In determining a schedule it might be found that, following the procedure outlined above, all the delivery dates could not be met or the loading on departments was very uneven when each job only moves onto the next department when it has been entirely completed. This might then involve a consideration of *split-batches*. Thus, for example, job 1001 might be split into two separate jobs 1001A and 1001B, with job 1001A being completed in department 1 in one week and 1001B in another week.

In manufacturing for stock the requirements are known before the planning period starts. With manufacturing against customers' orders this would only be the case if the orders were received well ahead of production starting and the production time-cycle was long. This might not be the case. In such a situation scheduling and loading cannot be more than an estimate of what is likely. The setting of delivery dates for new orders then requires careful consideration of the existing work loads and scheduling.

11.6.1 Loading schedule

The load is the work assigned to a machine or operator. The manufacturing schedule leads to the derivation of loading schedules. The aim of loading schedules is to make the maximum possible use of plant and personnel in the meeting of the target dates. Thus, for example, the manufacturing schedule which indicates in some week that jobs 1001 and 1002 will be completed in department 2 might then be broken down to indicate the loading for machine 1 of

Monday	08.30–17.00 Job 1001 Operation 1
Tuesday	08.30–12.30 Job 1001 Operation 1
	12.30–17.00 Job 1001 Operation 2
Wednesday	08.30–17.00 Job 1002 Operation 2
etc.	

11.7 Line of balance technique

The line of balance technique provides a method for the planning and monitoring of the progress with batches. Suppose we have a number of batches of components being processed, with each batch proceeding in sequence through a number of departments. How can we tell, in any one week or on any one day, whether all the work in each department

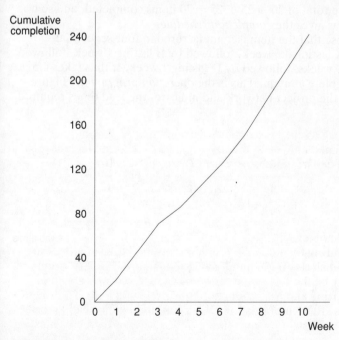

Figure 11.4 Completion schedule

Table 11.2 Job completion requirements

Week	Completions required	Cumulative completions
1	20	20
2	25	45
3	25	70
4	15	85
5	20	105
6	20	125
7	25	150
8	30	180
9	30	210
10	30	240

is going according to schedule so that the finished product will be ready in the right quantities in future weeks?

Table 11.2 shows a situation where different batch sizes have to be completed in each week. The required number of completions in each week is indicated and the cumulative number of completions required by any one week. Figure 11.4 shows a graph of how the cumulative completions are expected to vary with time. Thus, by the end of week 1 we should have 20 items completed, by the end of week 2 a cumulative total of 20 + 25 = 45 items completed, by the end of week 3 a cumulative total of 20 + 25 + 25 = 70 items completed, and so on. The graph thus gives the *completion schedule*.

Now suppose that the item is manufactured in four sequential operations: A lasting 0.5 week, followed by B lasting 1 week, followed by C lasting 2 weeks, followed by D lasting 1 week. It thus takes 4.5 weeks to complete an item. This is the *operation programme*. Figure 11.5 outlines the project network and indicates the lead times required

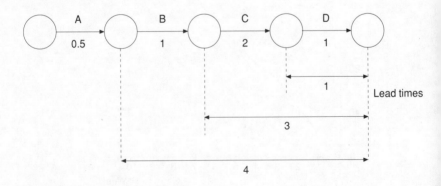

Figure 11.5 Operation programme

147

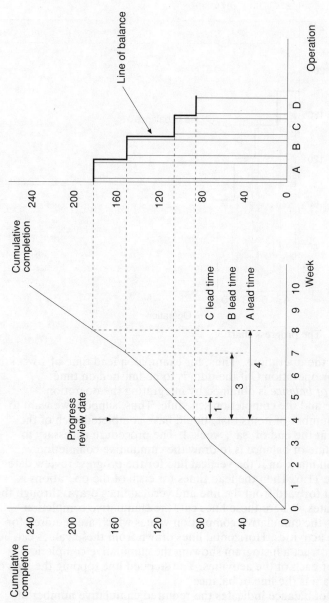

Figure 11.6 Construction of line of balance

148

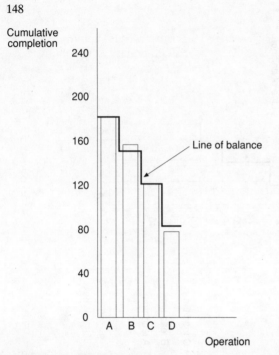

Figure 11.7   The progress chart

for each of the operations. Thus, for example, a lead time of 1 week is required for operation C if the item is to be finished on time.

The *line of balance* is obtained by integrating the operation programme and the completion schedule. Thus, suppose we want to know the number of items that should have completed each of the operations at the end of, say, week 4. The procedure necessary to obtain the line of balance is to draw the cumulative completion diagram and mark on it the vertical line for the progress review date, as in Figure 11.6. Then the lead times for each of the operations is stepped out forward from the line and vertical lines drawn through the resulting dates. Where these lines cut, the cumulative completion graph gives the cumulative completion values which are required for each of the activities. Horizontal lines drawn from these values can be used to construct a histogram showing the cumulative completion required for each of the activities. The stepped line topping the bars on the histogram is the line of balance.

The line of balance indicates the required cumulative number of items to have completed each activity if items are to be delivered in the required numbers on the required dates. If a histogram is drawn indicating the actual cumulative numbers of completions for each activity and the line of balance is superimposed on it, as in Figure 11.7, then the state of progress can be ascertained. Thus, for the progress chart shown in Figure 11.7, activity A is on schedule, activity B is ahead of schedule, activity C is on schedule, activity D is behind schedule.

Problems

Revision questions

1 Explain the effects on costs of batch size in the manufacturing of a component.
2 Derive an equation for the economic batch size for a product for which a company maintains no buffer stocks and delivers batches as an entity into stock.
3 A company has steady orders for 5000 of a particular item per year. What will be the economic batch size if the setting-up cost per batch is £300 and the holding cost per item is £6 per year? Assume that batches are manufactured and delivered in their entirety into stock.
4 A product is sold at the constant rate of 2000 items per month. The processing rate is 5000 items per month. If the setting-up costs are £30 per batch and the holding costs £0.05 per item per month, what will be the most economic batch size?
5 Explain the reasons that might arise for buffer stocks to be held.
6 For the data given in Table 11.3 for batches of different products, determine the sequence using (a) the first come–first served, (b) runout, (c) due date, (d) slack time, (e) processing time criteria.

Table 11.3 Problem 6

	Product				
	A	B	C	D	E
Sequence of arrival at work centre	1	2	3	4	5
Average demand/week	20	10	12	5	10
Current stock	80	40	60	30	60
Due date, week	4	2	3	1	6
Processing time in days	3	1	5	2	4

In each case state whether the product will be late and/or out-of-stock by the time the batch is delivered.

7 Explain how a schedule can be prepared by working backwards from completion dates.
8 Explain the circumstances under which split batches might be used.
9 Explain how the line of balance can be obtained and how it is used to determine the progress against a schedule.

Table 11.4 Problem 10: Delivery
schedule required

Week	Delivery required
1	15
2	20
3	25
4	25
5	25
6	20
7	15
8	10
9	10
10	15

Table 11.5 Problem 10: Activities involved in manufacturing
the product

Activity	Duration in weeks	Depends on
A	0.5	
B	1	
C	1	B
D	0.5	A
E	1	C and D
F	0.5	E

10 Tables 11.4 and 11.5 give the data for a product which is being
manufactured in batches. Determine the line of balance for week
4 so that progress towards achieving the required batches can be
determined.

Case problem

11 Company ABC is a small engineering company that is proposing
to change from making items to order to making items for stock.
It is recognised that there will need to be a policy determining
when batches should be ordered and the sizes of the batches.
Prepare a paper addressing these issues and indicating alternatives
that could be considered.

12 Flow production

12.1 Flow production lines

The term *flow production* is used to describe the production method involving discrete items being manufactured by progressing through a sequence of work stations on what is termed a production line. There are three basic types of such flow lines:

1 the *single-model* flow line, where only one product or model is made
2 the *multi-model* flow line, where batches of different products or models are produced in sequence on the same line
3 the *mixed model*, where more than one product or model is produced simultaneously on the same line.

With the single-model line the equipment setting and work allocation remains constant since there is no change in the product produced. With multi-model or mixed model there will be changes in equipment setting and work allocation as a result of changes in models or products. The greater the similarity of the work contents of the models or products, the easier it is to provide multi-model or mixed-model production.

12.1.1 Design of simple flow lines

The flow line consists of a number of work stations, each consisting of one or more machines and/or one or more workers. As the product travels down the line it becomes incrementally more complete at each station until, at the end of the line, there is the completed product. The total time taken to complete the product is thus the sum of the times spent at each work station.

The term *total work content* is used for the total time required to complete the product. Thus we can talk of the work content being divided among the work stations. The total work content is the sum of the total productive work time and the total non-productive work time, the term *non-productive work time* being used for time spent in handling and moving the product between work stations. The object in designing a flow line is to give an equal amount of work content to each work station. When this occurs the work proceeds smoothly with no hold-ups or build-ups from one work station to the next. This is known as *line balancing*.

If the work content at each work station is balanced as *t*, then for a line with *n* work stations the total work content of the line is

Total work content = Sum of *t* for the *n* work stations

Thus, for example, if there is a work content at each of 10 work stations of 20 minutes, then the total work content of the product is 20 × 10 = 200 minutes.

The time required to complete the work allocated to a work station is called the *service time* and the time available at each work station for the performance of the work is the *cycle time*. The cycle time is the time interval between the starting of work on successive items, or the completion of work on successive items. Thus if *N* items are produced by the line in a time *T* then the cycle time *C* is

$$C = \frac{T}{N}$$

The cycle time is normally larger than the service time, including some element of time for handling and movement of the product and idle time:

Cycle time = Service time + Idle time

and so

Cycle time = Productive work time +
             Non-productive work time + Idle time

The idle term occurs because it is generally not possible to balance the line so perfectly that each work station has an equal amount of work content.

The term *balancing delay* at a work station is the difference between the time available for a job and the time actually required, and is thus the difference between the cycle time and the service time for a work station:

Balancing delay = Cycle time − Service time

The term *balancing loss* is used for the balancing delay expressed as a percentage of the cycle time, i.e.

$$\text{Balancing loss} = \frac{\text{Cycle time} - \text{Service time}}{\text{Cycle time}} \times 100$$

The aim in designing a flow line is to have as low a balancing loss as possible, since this minimises the idle time.

12.2 Line balancing

The aims of line balancing can be considered to be that, for a given output rate from a line, the work elements should be assigned to work stations so that they:

1 minimise the idle time or balancing loss
2 minimise the number of work stations
3 spread the balancing loss as evenly as possible between work stations
4 conform to the constraints imposed on the sequencing of the work stations by the order in which processes are to be carried out and any others imposed by the way machines are grouped. (Such constraints are referred to as *precedence* and *zoning* constraints.)

12.2.1 Line balancing method

A simple approach to line balancing involves the following steps:

1 Identify (a) the number of work elements required for the manufacture of the product and (b) those that are to be completed by the flow line.
2 Draw a precedence diagram to indicate the precedence constraints on each of the work elements.
3 Calculate the cycle time and the minimum number of work stations.
4 Starting from the earliest work elements that are unaffected by any precedence constraints, determine the possible combinations which would give the required cycle time without violating precedence or zoning restrictions. This can then give the first work station.
5 Determine the next possible set of work elements which would give the required cycle time without violating precedence or zoning restrictions. This can then give the next work station. The process can be repeated until all the work stations have been identified.

To illustrate the above, consider a product having the 14 work elements outlined in Table 12.1. On the basis of the precedents indicated for each work element, the precedence diagram shown in Figure 12.1 can be drawn. With such a diagram a circle indicates a

Table 12.1 Precedence requirements

Work element	Duration in minutes	Depends on
A	5	
B	6	
C	7	
D	7	A
E	4	B
F	5	C
G	8	D
H	8	E and F
I	5	H
J	9	G and I
K	10	J
L	7	K
M	10	K
N	8	L and M

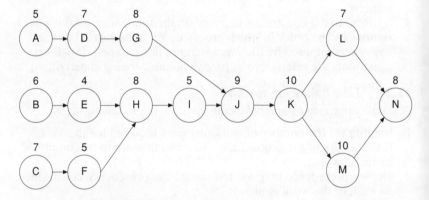

Figure 12.1 Precedence diagram

work element and the arrows drawn entering that element indicate the other work elements that must precede it. The work content, i.e. duration, of each element is indicated above the relevant circle. Thus, for example, work element A depends on no previous work element and has a duration of 5 minutes. Work element B depends on no previous work element and has a duration of 6 minutes. Work element J depends on work elements G and I having been completed and has a duration of 9 minutes.

Suppose a cycle time of 25 minutes is required. The total work content is the sum of the durations of each of the work elements and is thus

$$5 + 6 + 7 + 7 + 4 + 5 + 8 + 8 + 5 + 9 + 10 + 7 + 10 + 8 = 99 \text{ minutes}$$

Thus the minimum number of work stations is $99/25 = 3.96$ and so 4 work stations are envisaged.

If we start from those work elements which have no precedents, then in order to obtain a cycle time of 25 minutes we can consider the following combinations which do not violate precedence restrictions. It has been assumed that there are no zoning restrictions.

ABC   – cycle time 18 minutes
ADBC – cycle time 25 minutes
ABEC – cycle time 22 minutes
ABCF – cycle time 23 minutes
ADG   – cycle time 20 minutes
BECF – cycle time 22 minutes

Of these, ADBC gives the required cycle time and so might constitute the work elements for the first work station.

Effectively removing ADBC from the precedence diagram, we now have to determine the next set of work elements which would give the cycle time without violating precedents. Thus we might have

GEFH – cycle time 25 minutes
EFHI – cycle time 22 minutes

The combination GEFH gives the required cycle time and so can constitute the work elements of work station 2.

Effectively removing ADBC and GEFH from the precedence diagram, we now have to determine the next set of work elements which would give the cycle time without violating precedents. Thus we might have

IJK – cycle time 24 minutes

Since this is the only combination which does not violate precedents then this constitutes work station 3. This then leaves as the final work station

LMN – cycle time 25 minutes

The work elements at the four work stations are thus ADBC, GEFH, IJK and LMN. Apart from IJK there is no idle time. At IJK there is an idle time of $25 - 24 = 1$ minute.

The above represents a simple example of balancing an assembly line. Various techniques are available to assist with more complex assemblies and precedence rules. Some of the techniques are, like the method described above, rough trial and error methods, e.g. that developed by Helgerson and Birnie using ranked positional weightings (*Journal of Industrial Engineering*, XII No. 6, p. 394, 1961), while others are mathematical models based on queuing theory (see books on operational research for discussions of queuing theory, e.g. a simple

introduction is given by Makower, M.S. and Williamson, E.
Operational Research, Teach Yourself Books, Hodder & Stoughton,
1975). These mathematical models have been developed into computer
programs.

12.3 Production scheduling

With a single product or model, every item follows the same sequence
of operations from the first to the last in the line. Since each work
station will have the same cycle time the schedule is simple. Each work
station starts a new item every cycle and the finished items will emerge
from the last work station at the same cycle rate. Thus, for example,
for a flow line with four work stations and a cycle time of 25 minutes
the Gannt chart is as shown in Figure 12.2.

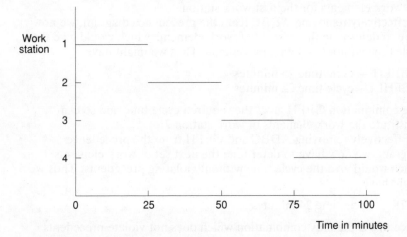

Figure 12.2 Gannt chart

With more than one product or model or batches, since all will
follow the same sequence through the work stations they will pass from
one work station to the next every cycle and the finished product will
emerge from the last work station at the cycle rate.

Problems

Revision questions

1 Explain what is meant by the terms *service time* and *cycle time* and
   explain why they might not be the same.
2 Explain what is meant by line balancing.
3 What are the objectives of flow line balancing?

4 A flow line has to produce 30 finished items per hour. The
   assembly of one item involves 20 elements of work and there is a
   total work content for an item of 12 minutes. What is the cycle
   time? What is the minimum number of work stations?
5 A flow line has to produce 10 finished items per hour. The
   assembly of one item involves 15 elements of work and there is a
   total work content for an item of 20 minutes. What is the cycle
   time? What is the balancing loss for the line?
6 The work involved in assembling a component can be described in
   terms of 10 work elements. Table 12.2 shows the work contents of
   these elements and their precedence constraints. Draw the
   precedence diagram and determine a possible production line
   which could produce the components at a rate of one every 12
   minutes.

Table 12.2 Problem 6

Work element	Duration in minutes	Depends on
A	4	
B	5	A
C	3	B
D	4	B
E	7	C
F	5	D
G	5	E
H	9	F
I	8	G
J	7	H and I

Case problems

7 Consider the components used in a mains electric plug (see Figure
   4.5) and the work elements involved in assembling the plug. Hence
   determine the precedence relationships of the work elements.
   Carry out an assembly and determine the work contents of each
   work element. Hence design a flow line to assemble such plugs,
   stating the output rate for which your line is designed.
8 Consider the work elements involved in the manufacture, from
   sheet metal of a case for some item such as a radio. Hence
   determine the precedence relationships of the work elements.
   Estimate the work contents of each work element and design a flow
   line to manufacture the case, stating the output rate for which your
   line is designed.

13 Inventory management

13.1 Inventories

The term *inventory* is used for items held in stock. The stock can be of

1. finished goods held waiting orders from customers
2. part-processed goods waiting for the next processing stage
3. consumable items such as materials which are bought-in for use in the manufacture of products
4. service materials that are used in such functions as administration and maintenance.

Among the reasons for having inventories are:

1. Finished goods stock may enable costs to be held down by permitting manufacturing in economic batch quantities (see section 11.2).
2. Finished goods stock may enable fluctuating customer demand, such as seasonal demand changes, to be met from less production capacity than would be needed to meet the peak demand. Finished goods stocks provide a buffer between the customer demand and the manufacturer's supply.
3. Some work-in-progress stock may be needed to adjust different rates of working between departments. Without such stocks all the manufacturing stages would need to be perfectly synchronised.
4. Work-in-progress stocks may enable production resources to be

used more economically.
5 Work-in-progress stocks may reduce delays due to defective work. With a production line operating without buffer stocks of work-in-progress, defective work could result in the entire line coming to a halt.
6 Consumable materials stocks may reduce production delays resulting from supplier delays in delivery or delivery of poor-quality material.
7 Consumable materials stocks and service materials stocks may permit items to be bought in quantities permitting of discounts or at favourable times.

13.1.1 Inventory costs

In general, the investment made by companies in inventories is large. A company can hold large stocks of work-in-progress, finished goods and raw materials. Inventory management to keep inventory costs down to the minimum level possible is thus important.

There are three main costs involved with an inventory:

1 The cost of ordering stock. This includes the purchase departments costs and might also include the costs of receiving the goods, quality inspection costs, and the costs of chasing overdue orders.
2 The cost of holding stock. This includes the rate of interest that could have been obtained from the capital if it had not been used to purchase the stock, all the costs incurred by storing the stock, deterioration costs, obsolescence costs, fire and general insurance costs.
3 The cost of running out of stock. This is a cost factor to take account of the loss of customer good will, changes in the market share, loss of future orders, etc.

The total inventory cost is thus the sum of the above three costs. Figure 13.1 shows in general terms how such costs might change as the size of the inventory is increased and how the optimum inventory level is that for which the total cost is a minimum.

13.2 Purchase or manufacturing orders

There are two basic ways by which purchase or manufacturing orders can be generated. These can be described as *stock point generation* and *order point generation*. With stock point generation the trigger which results in the issue of an order is the level of the in-company stock itself. With order point generation the trigger is an examination of the orders received for finished goods.

Stock point generation can work quite well when orders for finished goods are received at a reasonably constant rate and so the requirements for materials for production are reasonably constant. Methods of ordering with stock point generation are discussed in

160

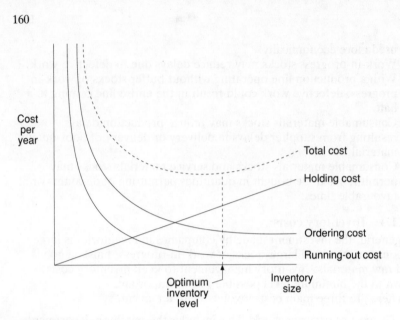

Figure 13.1 Inventory costs

section 13.3. Order point generation is necessary if the demand for finished products fluctuates widely. In such a situation purchasing or manufacturing orders are best linked to the orders received. One such method is known as *materials requirement planning* and is discussed in section 13.4.

13.3 Stock point generation of orders

There are two basic techniques with stock point generation:

1 Place an order when the level of the stock has dropped to some predetermined re-order level. The amount ordered is fixed and is just triggered by the drop to the re-order level. This is referred to as a *two-bin system*. The time interval between orders being placed is variable. This system requires continuous observation of stock levels.

2 Place an order at fixed intervals of time. This is referred to as a *periodic* or *batch system*. This system requires only periodic observation of stock levels. The amount ordered depends on the usage that has occurred and is often that which is required to bring the stock level back to some predetermined maximum level.

Figure 13.2 shows how the two systems compare in terms of the inventory level (or stock level)–time graphs. Figure 13.2(a) shows the same quantity being ordered every time the inventory level drops to the re-order level. With a variable withdrawal of stock the time

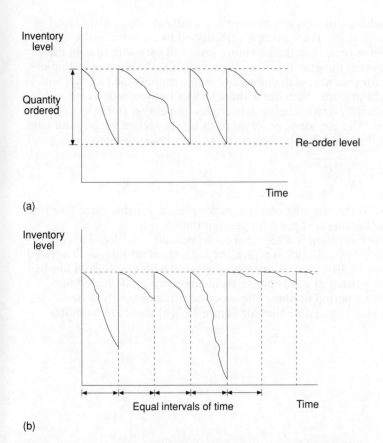

Figure 13.2 Inventory ordering systems, (a) two-bin, (b) periodic

between the orders is variable. Figure 13.2(b) shows stock being ordered at periodic intervals, the amount of stock being ordered being that required to bring the inventory level up to some maximum level.

The periodic order system has the advantage of being administratively more convenient since stocks are reviewed and orders placed at regular intervals. However, this method does lead to higher stock levels being maintained.

13.3.1 The economic order quantity

The *economic order quantity* (EOQ) is the quantity which results in the lowest total cost. It is usually derived as being the quantity for which ordering costs plus the holding costs are a minimum. The derivations are the same as those described in section 11.2 for the economic batch sizes, the economic batch size being the size of the batch which should be processed and hence delivered into the finished product store.

Consider a situation where there is a constant rate of withdrawal of items from stock. If the stock is replenished by an entire order being delivered at once then the inventory level will vary with time in the way shown in the graph given in Figure 13.3(a). This type of situation occurs, for instance, with commonly used materials such as nuts and bolts held in store. They are withdrawn at a fairly constant rate and replenished by a batch being delivered, as an entity, from the suppliers. The economic order quantity is (see section 11.2.1, and note that for Figure 13.3(a) no buffer stocks have been assumed)

$$\text{EOQ} = \sqrt{\frac{2C_s r}{C_h}}$$

where C_s is the ordering costs per order placed, r is the usage rate and C_h is the holding cost per item per unit time.

Another situation is where there is a constant rate of withdrawal from stock but the stock is replenished at a constant rate, as illustrated by Figure 13.3(b). Such a situation can occur with the stock of finished goods as a batch of goods produced in-company are delivered into store over a period of time. The economic order quantity is (see section 11.2.2, and note that for Figure 13.3(b) there are no buffer stocks)

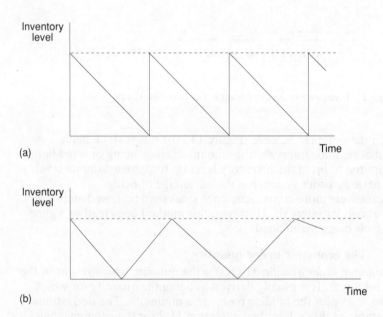

Figure 13.3 Inventory levels with constant demand when deliveries are (a) in complete batches, (b) at a constant rate

$$EOQ = \sqrt{\frac{2C_s r}{C_h(1 - r/q)}}$$

where q is the rate at which the stock is replenished.

Thus with the two-bin order system, if the rate of usage is perfectly constant then the stocks can be allowed to fall to zero and the quantity to be ordered can be determined by the use of the above equations. However, this ideal situation rarely occurs. The rate of usage might not be absolutely constant and the delivery time might not be instantaneous. Orders are likely to have to be placed some time ahead of the required delivery time to allow for the lead time of the supplier. There is thus a risk that the stock might be prematurely exhausted. For this reason buffer stocks are usually maintained.

With the periodic order system and the constant rate of usage, the optimum order interval will be

$$\text{Optimum order interval} = \frac{EOQ}{\text{Usage rate}}$$

Thus, for the situation where deliveries to stock are in complete batches

$$\text{Optimum order interval} = \sqrt{\frac{2C_s}{rC_h}}$$

When the deliveries are over a period of time, then

$$\text{Optimum order interval} = \sqrt{\frac{2C_s}{rC_h(1 - r/q)}}$$

13.4 Materials requirement planning

When the demand for a product is erratic, determining stock orders by stock point generation can result in problems. Such a situation might arise with batch manufacture when certain components or materials are required in large quantities at the infrequent intervals at which a batch of a particular product is made. In such circumstances it is more appropriate to generate orders by a method based on the numbers of orders for finished goods that have been received. The stock levels can then be geared to when a batch is to be produced and avoid stocks of components and materials being maintained at all times. Materials requirement planning is such a method.

Materials requirement planning is based on a bill of materials and the production or assembly schedule for a product. The *bill of materials* lists all the components and materials required for a product and the production or assembly schedule states when the components and materials will be required. Combining this information with a

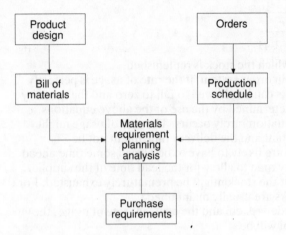

Figure 13.4 Materials requirement planning

knowledge of the lead times for delivery of components and materials from suppliers, enables the purchase dates for components and materials to be determined. Figure 13.4 illustrates this basis of materials requirement planning. The aim of materials requirement planning is to enable stocks of components and materials to be available for production when and in the quantity required, and otherwise, to keep inventories low.

Where a company is concerned with the production of many products by batch production, and if each product contains many components and materials, then the data-processing requirements involved in materials requirement planning can be considerable. The advent of computers for doing such tasks has, however, enabled this method to be more widely used than otherwise would have been the case.

13.5 Just-in-time

The inventory policy often adopted with many companies can be considered to be just-in-case buying and build up of stocks. Such a policy is one of not being sure what the demand will be and so of trying to make certain that whatever the circumstances there will be no running out of stock and machines and operators must be kept fully working. An alternative policy, which has been developed in Japan, is *just-in-time* (JIT). This is a manufacturing system which aims to have tight control of inventories. It works on the principle that components should not be made before they are required, and materials should not be ordered before they are required.

The manufacturing system consists of a series of small work units with each delivering from one to another in the successive stages of manufacturing. The line of work units is balanced so that each operates to a cycle of one day. What happens is that each work unit delivers to the next work unit the part-processed goods it needs for its production the next day. No greater accumulation of part-processed goods than one day is allowed to accumulate between work units. A work unit will have to cease working if this is going to occur. At the end of the production line the finished goods enter a store. Only when goods are withdrawn from this store can the last work station produce another batch. Thus each work station produces goods just-in-time for the next stage of production or delivery to the customer. The inventories of work in progress are thus kept to a minimum.

Such a system requires small batches to be economically handled. This requires changeover times between batches and setting-up costs to be kept low. To this end flexible machines with special equipment, and specialised staff, to aid in setting up tend to be used. Plant must be subject to a high standard of planned maintenance to minimise breakdowns.

The suppliers of materials and bought-in components must also be equipped to produce and deliver just-in-time. This requires a very close relationship between the manufacturing company and its suppliers.

13.6 Materials management

Materials management involves keeping track of all the materials, and components, in store. Three main documents are used:

1 *The materials requisition.* This document is the request to the stores to issue materials and, in addition to giving details of the required materials, it also gives details of who issued the order and to which cost centre the materials are to be charged.
2 *The purchase requisition.* This is the request for materials to be purchased. In addition to giving details of the materials, quantities and when required, it also gives details of who issued the requisition and to what cost centre the materials are to be charged.
3 *The stock record.* This is the record for each material or component, giving details of each material, its location in the stores, issues, purchases, minimum stock levels, maximum stock levels, order quantities and the stock balance at that time. The record thus lists all transactions involving the materials and so enables the up-to-date stock levels to be determined and decisions made with regard to re-ordering. Such records are increasingly being kept in computer files rather than on pieces of card.

The stock record for an item may include a column in which a running total of the total stock physically in the store is kept, with other columns indicating the date, the job references against which materials are withdrawn, and quantity withdrawn, as well as the reference of materials entering the store, the date and quantity. The running total is thus obtained by simply subtracting withdrawals and adding incoming stocks. Such a record indicates what is in stock but gives no clue as to whether immediate demands are going to be met. For this reason columns are sometimes included to give a record of what stocks are allocated against orders due in the immediate future. The deduction of these allocations from the initial stock enables what is termed the *free stock* to be identified. This is the stock for which no commitment has been made. A positive value for stock held in the store and a negative value for free stocks means that, unless more stock is introduced, the stock will shortly run out. The free stock value can thus be used as an indicator for when orders are required and may be better than basing re-ordering on the values of the stocks in the store.

The use of computers for stock control enables speedier recording and retrieval of data, the ability to handle forecasting methods for demand, speedier updating of inventory levels, speedier decisions with regard to stock requirements and other decision making, a reduction in the volume of documentation and tedious clerical work, a reduction in administration costs, and, because it can react more quickly and effectively to changes, the ability to operate with lower inventory levels.

Accurate stock records, whether on paper or computer, are essential if control is to be exercised over materials. The chance of errors is reduced if stores are secure – i.e. goods cannot enter or leave without an accurate and unambiguous record being made – and staffed by personnel who do storekeeping as a regular activity. Stocktaking can be used to update and correct stock records.

The duties of a storekeeper include the receiving and storing of materials, ensuring that the materials are stored in accordance with regulations, issuing goods only against authorised requisitions, maintaining stock records, and carrying out stocktaking to check what is held in store against what the stock records indicate. A goods inwards department is likely to be used to record the receipt of goods as they arrive, unpack them, check them against the original order, see that the goods are inspected to be of the right quality, return defective goods, inform purchasing and materials control departments of the receipt of the goods, and transfer the goods to the stores.

For a more detailed discussion of materials management see Barker, T., *Essentials of Materials Management*, McGraw-Hill, 1989.

13.7 Materials storage

There are many different types of stores that might exist in a company. For example, there can be

1 production stores containing the equipment, components and

materials needed for production
2 finished goods stores containing the completed products awaiting dispatch to customers
3 stationary stores containing the stationary items needed for administration within the company
4 special stores containing those materials, such as solvents and petroleum, which require special treatment because of fire hazards or other safety considerations.

The materials and components will be stored according to some stock location system. They might, for instance, be stored so that the same item is also stored in the same place. This method has the advantage that store staff become familiar with the fixed locations and so can rapidly find items. Locations might be specified by item classifications and coding references (see section 4.1.1). There is, however, the disadvantage that the store space might not be economically utilised if there is not a regular and constant flow of items. Another method of stock location might be termed the *random location* method. With this method an item is stored at different locations at different times, the location being determined by the next available space. The stock records are used to record where stock is located and thus need to be consulted when stock is to be issued from store. This method enables a more economic use of space than the fixed location method and is particularly suitable for automated stores.

The methods of storing items might be on shelving, in bins, on racking, on pallets, etc. Pallets exist in many forms from basic platforms to box structures and provide the facility for easy pick up and movement by fork lift trucks. They are often used as a means of collecting together a number of items and moving them as a single load. One of the aims with stores is to maximise the use of the floor space and building height in the store. Thus materials are likely to be stored both horizontally and vertically. Materials handling equipment may be used to enable materials to be not only easily moved but also easily stored and retrieved. Thus, for example, there are fork lift trucks which can operate within the narrow aisles between racks of materials, turn through 90° to store or retrieve goods from racks, and have a high reach so that goods can be stored to quite significant heights. Many attachments are available to enable drums, cartons, paper rolls, etc., to be handled. Cranes and conveyors are other examples of mechanical methods of handling materials.

Problems

Revision questions
1 Explain what is meant by the term *inventory*.
2 State the reasons for having inventories.
3 Explain the components of inventory cost.

4 Explain the operation of the two-bin ordering system.

5 Derive an equation for the most economic order quantity for an inventory where a store is involved and materials are delivered in batches.

6 Derive an equation for the most economic order quantity for an inventory where a finished goods store is involved and finished goods are delivery to the store at a steady rate.

7 Explain what is meant by a just-in-time policy of manufacturing.

8 List different types of store that may occur in a company.

9 What are the purposes of (a) a materials requisition document, (b) a purchase requisition document and (c) a stock record card?

10 Explain the differences between fixed and random methods of stock location in a store.

11 Explain the importance of accurate stock records.

Case problems

12 Prepare a bill of materials for a mains electric plug (see Figure 4.5 or take a plug apart yourself).

13 Company FGH manufactures, for stores, racking and wire basket containers which fit the racks. The racking is manufactured from lengths of a standard section of galvanised steel and the wire baskets are bought-in by the company as complete items. The racking material is supplied in packs which can be bolted together to form both the vertical and horizontal members of the racks. There are three standard packs: for the 1 m rack, the 2 m rack and the 3 m rack. The 1 m rack requires 10 m of section, the 2 m rack requires 24 m of section and the 3 m rack requires 37 m of section. The 1 m rack is supplied with 12 nuts and bolts, the 2 m rack with 20 nuts and bolts, the 3 m rack with 30 nuts and bolts. The baskets are supplied in three standard sizes, termed small, medium and large. The standard 1 m rack has three small baskets, the standard 2 m rack has four small baskets and two medium baskets, the standard 3 m rack has six small baskets, four medium baskets and two large baskets. The production department can produce at the rate of 100 of the 1 m packs per day, or 80 of the 2 m packs per day, or 60 of the 3 m packs per day. An allowance of 10 per cent has to be made for scrap with the work involved with the galvanised steel section.

(a) Draw up a bill of materials for the three standard racking packs.

(b) The company has decided to plan for steady requirements for 100 of the 1 m packs per week, 200 of the 2 m packs per week and 120 of the 3 m packs per week. Table 13.1 shows the current stock levels of materials and the lead times needed for fresh stocks to be obtained. Draw up an assembly schedule and a materials requirement plan, indicating clearly the size of orders to be placed and when.

Table 13.1 Problem 13

Item	Current stock	Lead time in weeks
Galvanised steel section	3000 m	2
Nuts	1000	1
Bolts	1000	1
Small baskets	1500	3
Medium baskets	1200	3
Large baskets	1000	3

14 The management of company STU, an engineering company which mass produces a small range of car engines, is concerned at the decrease in net earnings of the company despite an increase in sales. It is thought that a significant part of increase in costs can be attributed to inventory costs arising from the production line having buffer stocks between each of the main processes, the stores maintaining a buffer stock against the possibility of running out of stock, and the large stocks of some of the range of finished goods while others are understocked and there is a waiting period before orders can be met. Produce a reasoned paper outlining ways by which the problem can be tackled and the optimum level of inventories determined.

Appendix: Assignment-based learning

This topic of production planning and control lends itself to assignment-based learning. One possibility is thus, as a paper exercise (or on a computer screen), to consider a company manufacturing some product and then relate all the various parts of this book to it in terms of assignments to solve problems relating to that company. An alternative is to link this topic with the teaching of manufacturing technology, and perhaps other units such as materials technology, and have an integrated block of assignments linked with the actual production of some product in a simulated company context. The following set of assignments indicate how the assignment-based learning might occur for primarily the production planning and control topic.

Context

Consider all the following assignments in the context of an engineering company which might be set up by the college in which you are studying, with the college staff and the students forming the workforce. The company is planning to manufacture tool kits for car owners (or some other item which involves not too many components in order to keep the assignments to manageable levels).

The following are considerations, in relation to the chapters in this book, which need to be taken account of in determining the form of the company, its production organisation, and issues pertaining to the product. In each case you are expected to present reasoned arguments which you could justify to others (perhaps as a presentation to a 'manager' or the 'board'). At the end of the sequence of assignments you should have a completely worked out plan for production and its control.

1 Develop a structure for the company, taking into account the need for effective communication and control (Chapter 1).
2 Develop either an information system for the control and decision making in the company, based on paper or involving a computer (Chapter 2).
3 Determine the type of production operation that will be required and the consequential layout of plant (Chapter 3). You might be able to consider computer-aided engineering.
4 Determine the form of the product. This could be linked with computer-aided design in the production of a design for the product. This could also be linked with a materials technology unit and the selection of materials required for the product considered. Determine a parts list for the product and specify a part coding system, make decisions on 'make or buy' for each part, consider variety control, and use value analysis (Chapter 4).
5 Determine how quality control will be exercised in the company, developing inspection and statistical quality control plans (Chapter 5).
6 Develop designs for the workplaces and carry out studies on work methods in order to develop efficient working practices (Chapter 6).
7 Write job descriptions for the production workers (Chapter 6).
8 Design a market survey which could be used to obtain, prior to product launch, forecasts of demand for the product (Chapter 7). You might also carry out the survey among fellow students and analyse the data.
9 Develop a demand forecasting method which could be used when the product is in production (Chapter 7).

You might find it convenient, in the absence of any real data, to invent some data which can then be used as the basis for the remaining assignments.

10 Plan the capacity for the production, explaining how capacity might be adjusted (Chapter 8). Is the demand likely to be seasonal?
11 Carry out a project network analysis for the processing of the product. Consider whether resource levelling will be required. Produce a Gannt chart for the process. You might be able to use a computer program to aid in this (Chapters 9 and 10).
12 Determine the minimum cost batch (Chapter 11).
13 Determine a schedule for batch production (Chapter 11).

14   Set up a line of balance method for the monitoring of the progress of batches (Chapter 11).
15   Plan the flow line and balance it (Chapters 11 and 12).
16   Determine an inventory management plan (Chapter 13). For example, what will be the economic order quantities for components and materials? Consider materials requirement planning. Consider just-in-time. Consider whether you can carry out inventory management by means of a computer program.
17   How will raw materials, work-in-progress and finished goods be stored? Devise a storage plan (Chapter 13).

Further reading

The following text can be used to amplify particular issues. Within the text, references have been made to some of these texts and standards.

General extension of production planning and control concepts:
Hill, T., *Production/Operations Management*, Prentice-Hall, 1983.
Lockyer, K., Muhlemann, A. and Oakland, J., *Production and Operations Management*, Pitman, 1988.
Waters, C.D.J., *A Practical Introduction to Management Science*, Addison-Wesley, 1989.
Wild, R., *Essentials of Production and Operations Management*, Holt, Rinehart & Winston, 1980.

For management information systems:
Flynn, D.J., *Information Systems Requirements: Determination and Analysis*, McGraw-Hill, 1992.

For quality control:
Caplen, R.H., *Practical Approach to Quality Control*, Business Books, 1982.
Holmes, K., *Implementing BS 5750*, PIRA International, 1991.
Oakland, J.S., *Statistical Process Control*, Heinemann, 1986.

174

For operational research:

Burley, T.A. and O'Sullivan, G., *Work Out Operational Research*, Macmillan, 1986.

Lockyer, K.G., *Critical Path Analysis and Other Project Network Techniques*, Pitman, 1984.

Makower, M.S. and Williamson, E., *Operational Research*, Teach Yourself Books, Hodder & Stoughton, 1975.

For work study and work measurement:

Currie, R.M., *Work Study*, Pitman, 1986.

Whitmore, D.A., *Work Measurement*, Heinemann, 1980.

For materials requirement planning and management:

Barker, T., *Essentials of Materials Management*, McGraw-Hill, 1989.

Jessop, D. and Morrison, A., *Storage and Control of Stock*, Pitman, 1986.

Orlicki, J., *Materials Requirement Planning*, McGraw-Hill, 1975.

Answers to revision questions

The following are terse outlines of the answers to the revision questions in each chapter. To provide a proper answer they would generally need some expansion.

Chapter 1

1 To show the lines of authority within an organisation.
2 Authority can be delegated but responsibility cannot.
3 Vital for efficient running. Reducing length of line along which communications pass, e.g. decentralising, layout changes, group layout.
4 Planning, organising, co-ordinating, controlling, leading, staffing (see 1.3).
5 Targets, rules or procedures, supervision, grouping (see 1.3.1).
6 Planning, communicating, measurement, comparison, reporting, corrective action (see 1.3.2).

Chapter 2

1 To ensure actual performance meets that planned and to be able to make adjustments to enable plan to be achieved.
2 The control process involves planning and communicating the requirements, measuring performance against the planned

requirements and identifying deviations so that corrective action can be taken.

3   (a) Superiors and subordinates jointly set targets and periodically assess progress towards them. (b) Only significant deviations from targets are brought to a manager's attention.

4   (a) Tight, (b) loose, (c) loose.

5   A computer-based system which integrates all or most of the organisation's information systems and monitors activities throughout the organisation.

6   Manual involves paper returns being gathered in, processed by clerks, information extracted by them and put into a suitable form by management. Computerised can involve direct inputting of information at the information source, an ability to handle a much larger volume of data and a much higher extraction and presentation of information.

Chapter 3

1   Production planning and control, production, inspection, engineering, work study, maintenance, liaison (see 3.1).

2   Project – large-scale, unique; jobbing – one-off or small number of unique items; batch – batches of items produced; flow – production line; process – continuous production (see 3.2).

3   (a) Jobbing, (b) flow, (c) project, (d) batch.

4   (a) Jobbing and to a lesser extent batch, (b) as (a), (c) flow and to a lesser extent batch, (d) as (c), (e) as (c), (f) as (c). See Table 3.2.

5   Process – all plant associated with a particular process grouped together, jobbing and batch; product – plant in sequence of processes required by product, flow and process; group – plant grouped to deal with the characteristics of a particular family requiring similar processes, batch.

Chapter 4

1   Sequential – each drawing coded sequentially; product – parts coded to indicate the product for which they are designed; design – all parts coded according to some general code, the code indicating the nature and characteristics of the part (see 4.1.1).

2   To keep variety to a minimum. Benefits – savings in design costs, less variety of bought-in items, discounts for larger quantities of standard items, longer production runs with consequentially less setting-up costs, simpler production control, concentration of marketing effort, easier after-sales service (see 4.3).

3   Simplification – reduction of unnecessary variety; standardisation – control of necessary variety (see 4.3).

4   Determine total income generated by products, put products in rank order and determine accumulated income for successive

products, calculate percentage of income for these accumulated incomes, plot a graph of percentage accumulated income against percentage of range of products (see 4.3.2).
5 See Figure A.1.
6 Development, growth, maturity, decline (see 4.5).
7 An organised and systematic way of determining how the required performance can be obtained at the lowest cost without affecting quality (see 4.6).

Chapter 5

1 The totality of features and characteristics of a product or service that bear on its ability to meet stated or implied needs, i.e. fitness for purpose.
2 They have been issued with a certificate by a government-accredited certification company as conforming to the standard laid down in BS 5750 and are being periodically reassessed to ensure conformance.
3 As per BS 5750: Part 1. The sequence of operations required for production and the quality controls over the process, how the quality system is to work; how the requirements of the standard are to be met; quality procedures; quality responsibilities; quality checks – how, by who, when.
4 Product design quality is a measure of how well the design specification of a product meets the customers' design requirements. Product manufacture quality is a measure of how well the manufactured product conforms to the design requirements.
5 Failure costs, prevention costs, appraisal costs (see 5.3.1).
6 The highest percentage of rejects in a batch which the receiver of the goods will regularly accept.
7 The producer's risk is the chance that a batch will be rejected when the actual percentage of defective items is low enough for acceptance. The consumer's risk is the chance that a batch will be accepted when the actual percentage of defective items is high enough for rejection.
8 With a single sampling plan the decision as to whether to accept or not is taken on the basis of the inspection of a single sample. With double sampling a sample is taken and if the number of defective items is less than some number the batch is accepted, if greater than some other number it is rejected and if between these numbers a second sample is taken and rejection or acceptance determined on the basis of the number of defective items in this second sample.
9 Control by attributes is on the basis of right or wrong decisions, by variables on the basis of some property that varies.
10 0.107, 0.027, 0.0067, 0.0017.

178

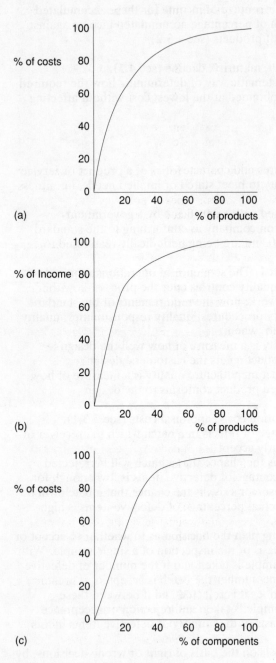

(a)

(b)

(c)

Figure A.1 Chapter 5 Problem 5

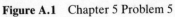

11 (a) Take action, (b) take a further sample as a check, (c) no action required.
12 $\bar{x} \pm 5.84, \bar{x} \pm 3.7$.
13 1.6, 23.4, 3.7, 18.1.
14 100.52 ± 1.27, 100.52 ± 2.01, 0.846, 8.906, 1.693, 6.932.

Chapter 6

1 The study of man–machine and man–environment systems.
2 (a) Signal light, (b) analogue display, (c) switch, (d) digital or analogue displays.
3 (a) Rotary or joystick selector switch, foot pedal, (b) handwheel or as in (a), (c) push button.
4 Foot pedals – force, speed; steering wheel – accuracy and to some extent range; gear stick – accuracy, speed; light switches/levers – ease of use, on–off.
5 To enable faults or interruptions to the line to have no immediate effect.
6 Method study – the development of efficient work methods (see 6.3). Work measurement – the application of techniques designed to establish the time for a qualified worker to carry out a specified task at a defined level of performance, for use in planning and allocating plant and labour workloads, setting standards, basis for incentive schemes, costing, comparing methods of working (see 6.4).

Chapter 7

1 Short – expected demand for products and so requirements for materials; intermediate – personnel, equipment, materials requirements; long – general future of company, e.g. product mix, new products, capacity changes, plant location (see 7.1).
2 See 7.2.
3 Drawing trend line, simple and weighted moving averages, exponential moving averages (see 7.3).
4 Simple moving averages give equal weight to all the data points, weighted ones do not and are useful when the latest data is more significant than older data.
5 4: 367, 5: 400, 6: 417.
6 (a) 4: 25, 5: 26, 6: 26, 7: 27, 8: 30, 9: 30, 10: 31, 11: 30, 12: 29, (b) 7: 26, 8: 27, 9: 29, 10: 29, 11: 29, 12: 30.
7 (a) 1: 500, 2: 500, 3: 495, 4: 503, 5: 553, 6: 603, 7: 643, 8: 684, 9: 726, 10: 787, 11: 787, 12 : 813, (b) 1: 500, 2: 500, 3: 485, 4: 493, 5: 645, 6: 752, 7: 826, 8: 908, 9: 951, 10: 996, 11: 997, 12: 1014.
8 $S = 10.12A - 3, S = 503$.
9 $S = 0.0116U + 20.67, S = 22.3$.

Chapter 8

1 Resources available for production processes, time available in a specified time/time to make one unit.
2 The capacity of the line is that of the smallest capacity process.
3 *nhsd/p*.
4 (a) Overtime, introduce shift working, hire staff, use part-time labour, subcontract work; (b) cut overtime, stop shift working, lay-offs, fire staff, drop part-time labour and subcontracting. See 8.2.1.
5 Chase demand or level capacity strategies, differential pricing, complementary products (see 8.2.1).
6 Allow stock levels to change, allow orders to build up or turn orders down.

Chapter 9

1 Activities, precedence relationships for activities.
2 Activity – a time-consuming task; event – a point in time.
3 A dummy activity consumes no time and is used solely for convenience in network construction.
4 See section 9.3. Earliest start and finish times working out from start, latest start and finish times working backwards from end.
5 Latest finish time for an activity minus the earliest start time for it minus its duration.
6 The longest duration path connecting the start and end events.
7 See Figure A.2.
8 See Figure A.3.
9 See Figure A.4.
10 See Figure A.5.
11 The activities are plotted against a time scale (see 9.4).
12 See Figure A.6.
13 See Figure A.7.

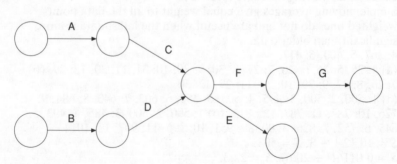

Figure A.2 Chapter 9 Problem 7

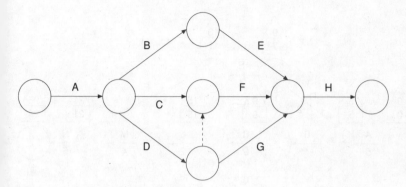

Figure A.3 Chapter 9 Problem 8

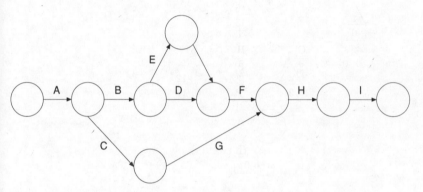

Figure A.4 Chapter 9 Problem 9

14 See 9.4.1.
15 In order to obtain a reduction in the time taken for a project at the least possible cost, the critical activity with the smallest cost–time slope is considered. The amount by which the duration can be reduced is determined by its crash limit. See 9.4.2.
16 (a) See Figure A.8, 21 days, critical path AFH, total cost 5380, (b) 20 days, 5370.

Chapter 10

1 Finished goods stocked and customers served from stock, goods made for stock and customers served from stock, goods made against customers' orders from standard materials, goods made against customers' orders with material having to be obtained. See 10.1.
2 Capacity planning, capacity adjustment, process planning. See 10.1.

182

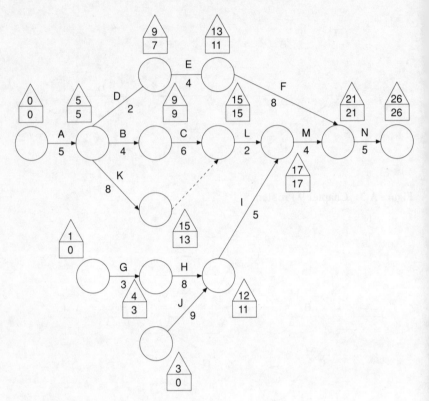

Figure A.5   Chapter 9 Problem 10

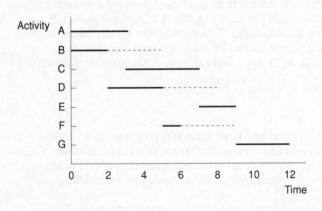

Figure A.6   Chapter 9 Problem 12

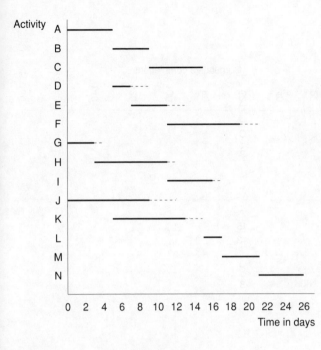

Figure A.7 Chapter 9 Problem 13

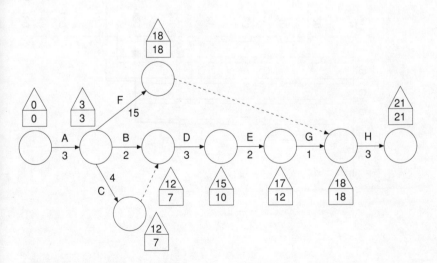

Figure A.8 Chapter 9 Problem 16

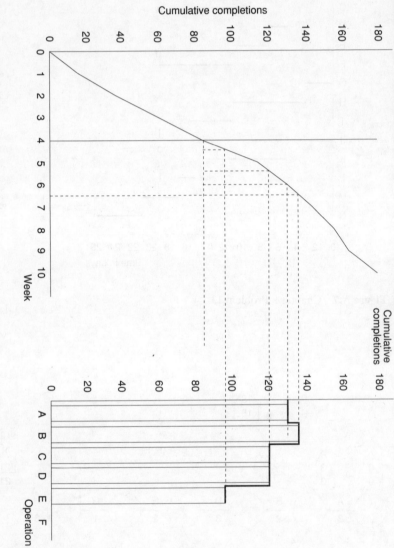

Figure A.9 Chapter 11 Problem 10

3 Capacity planning, capacity adjustment, forecasting.
4 If the materials required are non-standard then the sequence may be virtually the same as that given in 10.2.1, with A becoming discussion of required specification with customer. P, Q and T would not be required.
5 See 10.2. Actual times of events and activity durations can be plotted on a Gannt chart and compared with that required according to the network analysis.

Chapter 11

1 Batch sizes which are too small will result in the need for frequent processing and extra costs such as ordering costs, preparation and setting-up costs. Batch sizes which are too large will result in extra costs such as that due to the capital tied up in stock, costs of stock-keeping, depreciation.
2 See 11.2.1, EBQ = $\sqrt{2C_s r/C_h}$.
3 707.
4 2000.
5 See 11.3.
6 (a) ABCDE, (b) A/B, C, D/E, (c) DBCAE, (d) A/B/D, C/E, (e) BDAEC.
7 See 11.6.
8 When loading on departments was uneven or all the delivery dates could not be met.
9 See 11.7.
10 See Figure A.9.

Chapter 12

1 Service time – the time required to complete the work allocated to a work station; cycle time – the time available at each work station for the work. To allow some time for handling and movement of the product and idle time.

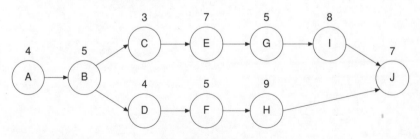

Figure A.10 Chapter 12 Problem 6

2   Adjusting the work stations in a line to divide the work as evenly as possible between them.
3   To minimise idle time or balancing loss, minimise the number of work stations, spread the balancing loss as evenly as possible, conform to sequencing constraints (see 12.2).
4   2 min, 6.
5   6 min, 17%.
6   See Figure A.10, work stations ABC, EG, DF, H, I, J.

Chapter 13

1   Items held in stock.
2   See 13.1.
3   Costs of ordering stock, holding stock, running out of stock (see 13.1.1).
4   Place an order for a fixed amount when the level of stock has dropped to some predetermined re-order level (see 13.3).
5   See 13.3.1, EOQ = $\sqrt{2C_s r/C_h}$.
6   See 13.3.2, EOQ = $\sqrt{2C_s r/C_h(1 - r/q)}$.
7   Manufacturing products and ordering materials only when the items are required (see 13.5).
8   Production stores, finished goods stores, stationary stores, special stores (see 13.7).
9   (a) Request to stores to issue materials, (b) request for materials to be purchased, (c) record for each material or component of stocks and location and all transactions.
10 Fixed – stock located according to some location system with the same materials always being in the same place; random – stock located according to space available and in no particular order or location.
11 For control to be exercised.

Index